SMALL CLAIMS

SMALL CLAIMS

JILL CIMENT

WEIDENFELD & NICOLSON
New York

Published by Weidenfeld & Nicolson, New York
A Division of Wheatland Corporation
10 East 53rd Street, New York, NY 10022

Library of Congress Cataloging-in-Publication Data

Ciment, Jill, 1953–
  Small claims.

  I. Title.
PR9199.3.C499S63   1986   813'.54   86-5463
ISBN 1-55584-000-0

Manufactured in the United States of America
by The Maple-Vail Book Manufacturing Group,
Binghamton, NY
Designed by Ronnie Herman
First Edition
10 9 8 7 6 5 4 3 2 1

For Arnold, Bernard and Gloria

Contents

SELF-PORTRAIT
WITH
VANISHING POINT

All the perspectives of my childhood converged on Miss Middleman, and when she announced there was going to be a drawing contest in my elementary school, I simply had to win. I was giddy with a confidence I had never before experienced, and never have since. The designated medium was crayons, a technique I felt particularly adept at.

I was sick in bed with chicken pox at the time, and reluctantly sent my mother to school to pick up my supplies. Now, the idea of my mother's walking into my classroom, speaking to Miss Middleman without my being there, without my strict young eyes guiding her in the protocol of first-grade etiquette, terrified me, but my mother somehow managed to rise to the occasion and appeared at my bedside holding out those bright crayons for my small spotted hands. For months afterward, whenever Miss Middleman mentioned parents in general, or politely asked after my mother in particular, I was terrified that she might mention some peculiarity. "Kim, is that your mother's natural hair color?"

My crayons included the usual colors, a sort of waxy rainbow. But what made me particularly fond of them was the line they produced, a cracked, tremulous line like adult handwriting. I believed they made my drawings look mature. I already had my subject matter planned—American football, something that seemed exotic in my Canadian childhood. In those years, I always searched for non-domestic subjects—horses, battles, sports—convinced that if I portrayed my real family with their idiosyncratic hysteria, I would be banished from the world of my bland peers. The football game I wanted to draw was unlike any football game I'd ever seen. There were to be no team players in my creation; each man would be out for himself. Like a ball game of braggarts, my players would be frozen in their most daring postures, ignoring everything else—the pigskin ball, each other, even winning—in order to be immortalized by my crayons. Of course, I simply assumed that their virtuosity would rub off on me, and spent the whole afternoon beginning my creation.

I don't believe that fever accompanies chicken pox, or any other physical discomfort except itching. It's as if your body falls victim to a form of social banishment; the hideous poxes, harmless in themselves, can be miraculously transferred, like wet, sticky red paint, onto all other children except those who have already shared your fate. Every morning I'd immediately scrutinize my limbs to see if the spots had vanished. I would study them with the same awe I'd bestow on a fading bruise, fascinated that my body, without my having urged it, could take it upon itself to erase the mistakes of a bashed elbow, a bruised knee.

Every day, with diligence—for even then I fathomed the unrelenting demands of my art—I'd work and rework my drawing until my ball players seemed to eclipse my illness, becoming indelible and bold even as I was fading back into normality. I filled in their faces, as children fill in the blank, jigsaw-puzzling shapes in coloring books (my only education thus far), until one morning, in a mysterious moment, a moment that even with age ceases to lose its mystery, I knew I was done.

At seven years old the satisfaction of bringing a task to completion was almost tactile. It was as if I'd been swathed in pride. But since I had just recently grasped the illusive nature of time—its implike trick of whisking away moments of pleasure while demonically stretching out seconds of drudgery—I was terrified to indulge in it. So I wore my pride sullenly lest it be snatched away. And in those long afternoons of recuperation, I picked at it as I habitually picked at the last clinging scabs of my illness. This, I believe, is how doubt linked up with the daisy chain of my childhood emotions.

My mother prided herself on being my emissary to the adult world and I in turn saw her as a phantasmagoric wedge into reality. She would be the first audience for my drawing. She professed to be the only one among her friends who knew how to raise children because she alone told children the truth. "I have always loathed your father, Kim, and have no idea why I'm alive." Later on, she explained, these truths would be the handles by which I could grasp reality.

I stood her in front of my drawing. Perhaps I hoped

that she might finally reveal what I secretly wished, that I was a child prodigy; that, unlike those gaunt, sallow little mathematicians who can untangle a knot of trigonometry before being able to tie their shoes, my secret, up until my illness, had been camouflaged from her by my healthy, ruddy looks.

"Do you want my honest opinion, Kim?"

"I guess," I said.

"I think you're going to win."

Although the gap between "win" and "prodigy" was immense, I was ecstatic.

"Do you really think so, mom?"

"I do," she assured me, "unless, of course, the contest is rigged."

Returning to school after a long illness is akin to being a minor celebrity. Standing in the playground with my drawing rolled under my arm, I answered all my classmates' questions about scabs, spots and the delectable habit of remaining in bed for hours. But even then, receiving adoration for what had accidentally befallen me (after all, I hadn't made my illness) left me bored.

Miss Middleman was my teacher and I revered her. A word from her, some absent-minded stare that singled me out from my restless classmates, left me dumbstruck. Yet I don't believe it was puppy love, but something deeper: a presence of inscrutable authority to whom I could bow down, and by doing so rid myself, once and for all, of the unbearable burden of my will. Her suggestions for classroom behavior were transformed by me into axioms. When she mentioned that all children should become right-handed, she cracked my ability to be ambidextrous, leaving me in this halved world where my left side has become a worthless appendage. Only once did my image of Miss Middleman falter. I was shopping with my mother on Saint Catherine Street when I spied Miss Middleman several store windows away. I was stunned. It seemed unbelievable that Miss Middleman would venture into the world and, perhaps even more astounding, shop. She had always worn the same sort of dress to teach in and I'd automatically assumed that it was an organic part of her, like hair. She began moving in our direction. In space the slight nudge of a meteor can cause a planet to careen light years off course and I, in my calculating panic, tried to bump my mother and deflect their eventual collision.

"Isn't the sidewalk wide enough for you, Kim!"

Miss Middleman was only yards away. I practically begged my mother to hide, when suddenly a miracle occurred. Two workmen carrying a store window sliced the sidewalk in two and we could only wave at her as though from one dimension to another.

"Did you notice her big black eye?" my mother asked as soon as she was out of earshot.

In my terror I hadn't registered anything. But now I could remember a slight bruise that, under my mother's influence, swelled to gargantuan purplish proportions.

"How do you think it happened, Kim?"

I reeled off a list of possible homemaking accidents.

"I doubt it," my mother said.

"How do you think it happened, mom?"

"Her boyfriend probably slugged her."

Imagine holding up a heavy glass pitcher while simultaneously knowing that you're going to drop it. Inevitably it does escape from your grasp, yet you continue to hold its shape forlornly in the air. In this way, I clung to my image of Miss Middleman.

As soon as I walked into the classroom, I presented her with my drawing. I unfurled it before her bespectacled eyes. Although I could easily decipher my own parents' expressions, which had a theatrical exaggeration about them—anger was literally bared teeth, sorrow was catatonic rocking—I was still unable to read the subtle hieroglyphics of most adult faces. I gazed uncomprehendingly up at Miss Middleman.

"This is very good, Kim," she said, "but what on earth do all these football players mean?"

To me they meant only one thing—the possibility of my winning the contest. But even at that age I knew the vanity of such an admission. I looked back down at my ball players. They were all fixed in their moment of glory and suddenly it occurred to me that I had simply rendered, with brash, indelible crayons, the undeniable evidence of my longing.

I prayed Miss Middleman wouldn't notice. I had no religious background and imagined God to be an all-seeing head, as enormous as a hydrocephalic's I'd seen in one of my mother's tabloids.

"Do you think you could articulate it to the class, Kim?"

"No."

"No?"

"No."

"Well, perhaps we shouldn't ask artists to explain their work," she said kindly.

I reeled around and sank into my assigned chair.

Up until that moment I had always felt that my being, what my mother called "that personality of yours, Kim," was safely trapped inside me. It might surge and roll around, ricocheting within the helmet of my skull, yet it could never escape. But now, seated in front of Miss Middleman, I felt porous and pregnable, as if the world could leak in—or worse, I could seep out. For the rest of the day I performed my written lessons by rote. But every now and then, if I thought I spied a trace of my personality creeping through, I'd rub it out into the pink ashes of my eraser and blow it away.

Whatever happens to me today can easily be tested in the laboratory of my past, but as a child those scanty years accumulating behind me seemed devoid of graspable matter. And so I tested things out on my mother. As soon as I got home from school, I ran through the house to find her. She was seated, as usual, in front of her vanity mirror, dismantling her platinum bouffant for its weekly peroxide treatment. Her hair of late had become extraordinarily thin and tufts of it, ensnarled in her comb, lay discarded on the counter. For a moment, I looked at her with a detachment I'd never experienced before. Hair, according to Miss Middleman, refuses to accept death. It continues to grow even after the heart has stopped and once, when she offhandedly mentioned this during a hygiene lesson, I came to believe that hair, above and beyond all our bodily organs, contained our souls. Miss

Middleman's hair was worn in a stiff knot. Mine was shorn off because I loathed combing it. But my mother's hair, now falling out from her peroxide treatments, was continually changing colors. Suddenly, a feeling of absolute and utter sadness came over me.

"What did Miss Middleman think of your drawing?" my mother asked.

"I guess she liked it," I said.

"You guess?"

"She wanted to know why I drew so many football players."

"What's it her business?"

"Oh, mom, I'm so worried that Miss Middleman thinks I only care about winning."

"Kim," my mother assured me, "I'm sure Miss Middleman doesn't give you a thought."

In the back room of the Musée de Montreal is an untitled still life that I worshipped as a child. For years I thought it was called *Untitled*. The apples, grapes, plums and oranges were rendered in remarkable detail, their stems had veiny leaves and some of their skins were glassy. But what entranced me was that each piece of fruit was frosted on one side, as if in perpetual winter, while the other half was drenched in the light of some invisible source. It made them look timeless, but not in the way my mother used timeless. "Grace Kelly's looks are classical because blond hair has a timeless beauty" or "Stop sulking about new clothes, Kim, saddle shoes are timeless!" These fruits in their seasonal shifting (for I truly believed they revolved imperceptibly around the axis of their stems) existed in sidereal time, and whenever the hours lurched and sagged for me—the winners of the contest were going to be announced the next morning—these fruits would remain the same, never decaying, but turning forever in the constancy of seasons.

That night I devoured my first fingernail (a taste that carried within its brittle texture a lifetime of craving) and early the next morning, dressed in my saddle shoes, I hurried to school. The competing drawings were going to be unveiled during our school assembly and I desperately wanted to see how mine would stack up against those of my peers. I took a seat in the first-grade section of the auditorium where children in various postures of anxiety squirmed in their chairs. I proudly remained stoic.

Miss Middleman tapped on the microphone and asked the janitor to roll back the curtain. For a moment, I scrutinized a whole panorama of childlike worlds halved by simple horizons. On top of the horizons were all things ethereal—clouds, sky and stars. The suns were strung up by their own rays. Below, weighted down by the gravity of subject matter, were parents, teachers (one of my classmates had done a portrait of Miss Middleman), houses, and my football players. But what astonished me wasn't so much the differences in these clumsily rendered worlds as their undeniable uniformity. These lopsided houses, crooked trees, spindly figures, were the saddest things I'd ever seen—no matter what we'd drawn, we'd all seen the world exactly the same way.

I suddenly wanted to cry. But Miss Middleman had once said we are made up mostly of water and a handful of chemicals, and I was terrified that if I did cry, I simply wouldn't stop, and then what would be left of me? According to Miss Middleman, there would be enough carbon to fill nine thousand lead pencils, a cube of sugar, one and a half bags of calcium, and enough phosphorus for just enough matches to illuminate the small place in the world I occupy.

ASTRONOMY

My plum, my sweet, you're all I've got, little pumpkin. So you've got to give me a straight answer. Darling, just tell mother the truth. Don't lie. Terrible things happen to children who lie."

Through a hole in the bathroom door the shape of her father's foot, the child listened dutifully to her mother's voice. Her mother had been locked in there since noon. It was the twenty-sixth consecutive Saturday that her mother had changed the color of her hair.

"Well, scrumptious, are you ready?"

The child nodded in agreement.

"I can't hear you!"

The child shook her head more vigorously.

"All right, plum, stand back."

The door burst open, and when her mother emerged the child sighed in relief. She still recognized her mother. Her hair was now in the shape of a rocket ship, the color of a carrot.

"Well?" her mother asked, sinking to her knees and bending forward. Then she scooped up her head in her large hands and offered it to the child like a beach ball.

The child simply stared. Every Saturday, to her total

dismay, her mother had demanded the same answers. How do you compare wheat blond to carrot, the color of the sun to moonlight tawny? Still, the child had become more sophisticated. She'd loathed last month's oo-la-la black.

"You'll tell mother the truth, won't you, little pumpkin?"

"I swear," the child swore.

"Do you think," her mother asked, "do you think I look younger?"

The child never knew what to say. She still thought of age in fractions; she was six-and-one-half going on six-and-three-quarters. She stared at the conical mass of orange projecting from her mother's head and tried thoughtfully to unpuzzle it with the complex logic of childhood; orange is younger than black, the shape of a rocket ship more spectacular than bangs.

"I think," the child said, "I think you look beautiful." And she meant it. Astronomy was her favorite subject in school.

Mother and child had earthly problems. They lived all alone in a streamlined trailer at the edge of the desert. The child's father had jettisoned himself out of their lives months ago.

"Tell me, little darling," her mother asked at breakfast, "what exactly are you learning in school?"

"The order of the planets," the child said proudly. She couldn't take her eyes off her mother's hairdo. During the night it had become even more projectile. A small clump had dislodged itself and now orbited around one ear.

"What about electricity?" her mother continued. "Are you learning anything about electricity?"

"Electricity?" the child said.

"Yeah, sweets," her mother said, "you know, bulbs, toasters, et cetera, et cetera."

"It's borne in our atmosphere," the child said proudly.

"A lot of good that does me."

"And they think," the child continued happily, "that other planets might have electricity too."

"Well, kid, I don't know how to break this to you, but if we don't get some money soon, we're not going to have any."

The thought of losing electricity was horrifying to the child. "What will we do?" she cried.

"I was hoping you'd know."

"Me, mom?"

"You're the scientist in the family."

"But, mom, I'm only a little girl," the child said. And to demonstrate this, she stood up.

"We could have you sweep chimneys," her mother teased.

"I'll do it," the child volunteered.

"There are no chimneys in a trailer park."

"I could do odd jobs."

"You're too little," her mother said, "and besides you're so clumsy."

"Oh, mom"—the child burst into tears—"I want to help!"

"Let's see," her mother said calmly. But she didn't look calm. There were now many clumps of hair toppling off the orange mass. The whole stiff cone was leaning to one side. A bobby pin jutted out of the top like an antenna. "When I was a little girl," her mother continued, "every Saturday and Sunday I used to go around and polish the neighbors' shoes."

"You did?" the child said. She was astonished. Her mother rarely left the trailer now.

"I wasn't always like this. I had a red wagon, just like yours, and I used to go from door to door."

"I could do that," the child said.

"I bet you could," her mother said. She absently lifted one of her large hands and attempted to straighten the sagging cone. "But of course," she quickly added, "you'd have to be willing to make an investment."

The child looked puzzled.

"Investment," her mother said. "Don't they teach you anything about investments in school? Don't they teach you anything practical? I'm going to have to have a word with your teacher."

Immediately the child pictured her mother pounding at the classroom door, its giant knob turning. Her assigned seat was in the last row and, over the cowlicks and pigtails of her schoolmates, she could see the door's window with its textured glass and ROOM 10 all spidery in reverse now ablaze with her mother's hair.

"I'll do anything, mom! Please, please don't come to my school!"

"All right, little pumpkin," her mother said, "run and get me your piggy bank."

The child ran and got her piggy bank.

"How much did you say you had in there, plum?"

"I didn't, mom."

They counted the coins together. They each came up with a different figure. The mother calculated on her bony fingers. The child closed her eyes and pictured tallies on the undersides of her lids.

"I suppose I'll have to take your word for it, kid," her mother finally sighed. Then she picked up her purse, snapped open its jaws and, scooping up all the child's coins, plopped them inside. "When you come home from school today," she assured her little girl, "I'm going to have a terrific surprise waiting for you."

The child never enjoyed her mother's surprises. As a matter of fact, they terrified her. Once, when the child announced there was going to be a total eclipse of the sun, her mother had made pin pricks in all the blinds. Another time, after the child gleefully described the planetarium she'd seen on a field trip, her mother had painted the child's bedroom black. Now, standing on the steps of their trailer, a tower of school books balanced in her arms, the child knocked nervously on the metal door. She couldn't reach the aluminum handle. Her mother was always there to greet her. But today the child heard rapid footsteps resounding through the trailer, and when the door finally creaked open her mother's hand emerged, signaling her inside.

"Surprise!" her mother said.

Immediately the child checked her mother's hair, scrutinizing it for changes. It was still flaming orange but the cone had now fallen into a sphere and looked very much like an illustration of centrifugal force.

"Not there, darling," her mother said, pointing downward, "here."

Strapped to her mother's feet were two garishly polished shoes. They had once been black, but now a streaked layer of pink rambled all over them.

"I don't understand, mom."

"Follow me," her mother insisted.

Down the narrow hallway, the child followed the shoes. On one heel, the base had been left untouched, like a black root. On the other, the color was so startling that it clashed with her mother's hair. They stopped in front of the child's bedroom.

"Well?" her mother said.

Peering around her mother's legs, the child saw her red wagon. It was parked under a lamp and scrubbed absolutely clean. Little bottles of new shoe polish were lined up along its front, and arching out of its back rose the loops of a metal shoe rack. Her mother had tied a ribbon around its handle and painted, in yellow shoe polish against its crimson side, SMART SAL'S SHOES AND SHINE.

"I hope you like it, Sally."

"Are you kidding?" the child said. She embraced her mother's legs.

Saturday couldn't come fast enough. Each morning at breakfast the child and her mother only discussed business strategies and how fast she'd be able to earn back her original investment. After that, of course, it was pure profit. Her school work slowly began to fall apart. Attending class was nothing but a loathsome burden. The big round clock over her desk ticked excruciatingly slowly. The teacher's voice came to her as if spoken under water. And once, when called upon, she got the order of the planets all jumbled up. The days dragged on one by one. Saturday, like a receding horizon, never seemed to materialize. And then, of course, it did.

"I'm ready, mom," the child announced. Scrubbed and clean, she stood in the door of their trailer waiting for her mother's inspection. Her little shoes were dazzling.

"You'll knock them dead, kid."

Together they lifted her wagon onto the sidewalk.

"Do you have everything?"

"Check," the child said.

"Good luck!"

"Do you think I'll need it, mom?"

"Of course not."

They winked, shook hands, embraced. Then, pulling her wagon behind her, the little girl hit the streets. But who in his right mind lets a six-year-old polish shoes? Doors were slammed on her in mid-sentence. Sometimes she had to communicate through a mail slot. Every now and then a friendly soul offered her lemonade, but quickly retreated with shoes still firmly on feet. Within an hour, the child was hopelessly depressed. She plopped down next to a gutter and burst into tears.

"What are you crying for, cry-baby, huh?"

It was Johnny Swat, an older classmate, tightrope-walking along her curb.

"I'm not," the child insisted.

"Then what *are* you doing?"

The child explained her business venture and the concept of investing.

"How boring," Johnny said. He was extraordinarily energetic. He listened to her profit projections while doing somersaults. Then he began reading off the labels of her shoe polishes. "Sunset Pink," he read, adding, "how hopeless." He suggested she follow him home.

"What for?" the child asked.

"You'll see."

As distraught as she was, the little girl picked herself up, responsibly dragging her wagon behind her. They entered Johnny's parents' garage.

"Take a look," he said.

On the hood of his father's car, baking in various jars, sat sun-stroked insects on wilting branches.

"It's my bug collection," he informed her. He led her to a corner. Here, with straight pins from his mother's sewing kit, he had impaled a number of species to his father's golf balls.

"I'm going to send one into space every day," he announced.

It was a horrifying sight. Moths flapped frantically, beating the color from their wings; rows of tiny legs writhed; and a beetle, turning and turning around the head of a pin, ran as if on a treadmill. The child couldn't take her eyes off it.

"Pick one," Johnny said.

Antennae twitched in every direction. Bending closer, the child was sure she saw terror in their compound eyes.

"Well?"

One caterpillar pinned twice, fore and aft, clung to the curvature of its golf ball. Although shoeless, it had a thousand feet.

"That one," the child said.

Johnny stooped over and scooped it up, careful not to squish it. Then he selected a golf club.

"Come along," he said.

Out of the garage and into the street, past all those doors where she'd cringed in terror, the child followed the bug and boy, dragging her wagon behind her. They teed up in a vacant field.

"Take one last look," Johnny insisted.

In close-up, as if the whole world consisted of this scene, the child scrutinized the caterpillar. Baking, pinned, exhausted, it seemed almost content. On top of the ball balanced on the tee, it slowly lifted its head as though simply to stretch. And a moment later, bug and ball were hurtling through the sky out of sight.

The child sat down. The horror of what they'd just done suddenly hit her. For a moment, she pictured the bug, antennae drawn back, sailing through cold space at an accelerated speed. Then she too was filled with the sensation of motion. Clinging to the ground, her world like a golf ball, she saw herself and her red wagon with its empty shoe rack being hurled through space in the opposite direction. The child was awe-struck. Nothing this important had ever happened to her. She clambered to her wobbly legs, grabbed the wagon's handle and, pulling it behind her, ran to tell her mother.

"Now I've gone and ruined your life too," her mother greeted her, staring at the empty shoe rack. She was sitting on the steps of their trailer with a beach towel wrapped around her head. The child plopped down before her and attempted to explain her revelation.

"Mom," she began, "we're no different than insects."

"You're telling me," her mother said.

With sweeping hand gestures, she described the bug and ball, the world and herself.

"Big deal," her mother said. She kept staring at the empty shoe rack.

"Oh, mom," the child insisted, "it doesn't matter now!"

"Oh yes it does," her mother said. "I'll give you revelations."

She bent forward, unwound the towel and exposed her head to her daughter. Very little hair was left. What remained had finally broken off and, here and there, only small clumps sprouted like seedlings.

The child didn't even notice the change of color. Under the direct sun, between the now-distinct roots, she could see the whole of her mother's skull—white, round, as fragile as a porcelain globe.

Her mother looked up.

"Don't you see me for what I am?" she asked her little girl. "Can't you see what I'm really like?"

"Yes," the child said honestly. Her mother didn't look too good now, but she thought she was beautiful.

GENETICS

The mice came out the wrong color. The child's experiment in genetic breeding for the Science Fair was a flop. She sat glumly beside her mother, cradling her head in her chubby hands.

"We could always touch up your mice with a little of my hair coloring," her mother suggested.

"Oh, mom," the child explained, "scientists aren't like that."

"If they aren't interested in winning or losing, then why did they call it the human race?"

She lifted the child onto her broad lap. She was a huge woman with a blond, helmet-shaped wig. Wisps of her own hair, the color of brass, stuck out the bottom like goose down.

"I just want to be a part of my darling's ambitions."

"Do you think it could work, mom?"

"Why not?" her mother said.

A bowl of black dye was prepared in the bathroom. The child, · with much trepidation, brought her mother the mice. They all ran up to the bars of their cage as if to volunteer.

"Well, at least someone's showing a little enthusiasm around here."

"Will you do it, mom?"

"Of course."

But as soon as her mother reached into the cage, the mice lost all sense of participation. They ran in mad circles and even the mother mouse, who normally swaggers in front of her brood inspecting them with the scrutiny of a drill-sergeant, now raced to the rear and, to save herself, actually used her paws to volunteer her startled sons into stepping forward.

"I can't watch," the child said.

"Then shut your eyes."

The child shut her eyes. Within no time, she felt a peck on her forehead.

"I'm through," her mother announced.

"Oh my God, mom, even their tails and teeth are black!"

The wet shivering mice panicked. That night their exercise wheel spun under their frantic feet. In the morning they had quieted down and by late afternoon, they'd fallen into a depressed stupor, lying around their cage like lumps of coal.

"I suppose they're out of commission for the Science Fair now," her mother said. She stood in front of the mice's cage weeping unabashedly. "I'm so sorry, Sally."

"Please, mom, forget it."

"I can't," her mother said. "I feel like I've ruined our lives."

"Oh, mom," the child assured her, "I'll come up with a new experiment."

"When?"

"How should I know?"

Her mother collapsed on the sofa.

"You've got to hurry, Sally, I'm growing old." Lifting a tremulous finger, she showed the child a whole new network of wrinkles. "Help me."

With ant-like energy, the child's mind ran up, down and sideways, trying to find a crumb of rational scientific information for her distraught mother.

Her mother lay prostrate before her. Under her nylons the prickly hairs of her huge legs were squashed like specimens under glass.

"Mom, please don't worry, the average American woman has sixteen square feet of skin."

What makes for the desirable offspring, the true egg amid a dozen look-alikes? Some laboratory hens, when confronted by a whole assortment of artificial eggs—square, oblong, triangular, flat—will opt for the largest, even if it's eight times the size of her normal output. Neglecting all others, she'll squat atop this gargantuan decoy, fussing and cooing grotesquely.

"Look here," her mother said, leafing through her favorite tabloid a couple of days later. "A two-headed snake was born at our zoo. I bet if you had a two-headed snake, you'd floor them at the Science Fair."

"I guess I would, mom, but—"

"But what?" her mother said. "There's no doubt about it, you'd be the toast of your class."

"Mother, after what happened with the mice?"

"I'd rather not talk about it," her mother said. She continued leafing through the pages, avoiding the child's eyes. Then, peering up over bold headlines all speckled with exclamation points, she said, "I just don't understand why you can't create a mutant by mating that pet rat of yours with one of the local rabbits."

"But mom, according to my teacher, mutations are caused during pregnancy by an exposure to either cosmic rays or x-rays."

"Is that all? Is that what we're making such a big deal about? I wish I had your problems."

"How can you say that, mom?"

"Well, I can always write a note to the school nurse saying that you've been exposed to tuberculosis. Just get your rat in a family way and slip it in your pocket during the x-ray."

"I couldn't do that," the child said, aghast. "What would the nurse say?"

"If you're not interested in creating a new life form—"

"You know I am."

"Well," her mother asked, "what would other successful scientists do? Do you think Einstein worried about his school nurse?"

"Of course not, mom."

Her mother chucked aside the tabloid, bent over, and scooped up the child in her huge arms. "Besides, darling," she said, "if it does work, we'll call the new species Sally's Strain!"

That afternoon the child made all the necessary arrangements. In exchange for pick of the litter, an older classmate, Johnny Swat, allowed his male rat to stud her female and the next morning, note in hand, rat in pocket, she posed for her x-ray. Immediately the child envisioned its pregnant cells exploding, chromosomes being whacked around, sugary strands of DNA pulled apart like taffy. Her brain was reeling with possibilities and, for a moment, in the laboratory of her mind, she saw baby rats with pointed heads, misshapen limbs, hooves, scales and tusks.

Twenty-one days later, her radiated rat groaned with birth pangs.

"Oh my God, it's time!" cried the child.

The rat had collapsed on its side. Its flanks twitched, its swollen stomach heaved and rolled like an inner sea.

Slamming the door so that her mother couldn't see her, the little scientist sank to her knees and irrationally prayed, "Please . . . please make monsters come out."

The rat gave birth to the usual wormlike infants—red, gummy and bald. After a couple of weeks they sprouted hair, grew claws, opened their veiny eyelids. None of them, however, displayed any physical abnormalities.

The child made note of everything. As a family unit, they had extremely poor hygiene; they rarely licked themselves, they grew slovenly, trailing dust and pellet crumbs from their whiskers and tails. When she tested them in a simple maze, they piled up in blind alleys. One afternoon, two mounted their exercise wheel and tried to run in opposite directions.

There was definitely something wrong with them.

"Maybe they're mental mutants," her mother suggested.

"Oh, mom, I just have to face it. They're morons."

"Well, that's certainly not a new life form."

The child racked her brain for a scientific explanation. Perhaps it was the lack of oxygen when the pregnant rat had been stuffed in her pocket?

"I don't remember anything about a rat being in your pocket, darling."

"How could you not remember, mom? It was you who suggested it!"

"Please don't get angry with me," her mother said tearfully. Then she grabbed hold of the child's head and buried it in her ample breasts. "Do you think I'm losing my memory, Sally?"

What is memory and where does it go?

Her simpleton rats were abandoned on the shelf next to her dyed mice and, for the child's next experiment, she collected flatworms. As everybody knows, worms can regenerate. Lop off their heads with a hoe blade and they'll just sprout new ones. That evening she mixed a solution of mud, moss and water in her mother's hair coloring bowl, dropped the worms in and began the methodical task of training them.

"Is this absolutely necessary?" her mother asked.

"Yes," the child said.

With her school pencil, she poked ruthlessly at the worms until their tortured bodies contracted in terror.

Eventually all she had to do was wield her pencil and the worms curled up like anchovies.

She explained the whole thing to her perplexed mother.

"Since worms have a more regenerative nervous system than yours, mom, we can discover how retention works. The question is whether the memory of the pencil will remain in their headless bottom halves."

"I'd rather not know," her mother said.

The child took out a steak knife and sliced the worms in two. They then required a dark moist place for their regrowth, so she selected the bathroom drawer.

A couple of weeks later the bowl was missing.

"Where are my worms, mother!"

"Outside. I couldn't bear to have them near me."

The bowl sat baking on the back stoop. All the water had evaporated and the mud had now dried into a hard solid brick. With a hammer and screwdriver, the child chiseled away frantically, excavating her worms.

These flatworms, unlike ants, had had absolutely no sense of community; they kept to their own patch of dirt and would sooner have starved than share a morsel of moss. Even sliced in two, they didn't bother to rub up against their former selves. But when their world suddenly began to harden like brick around them, they gushed with sentimentality. Then they rubbed up against one another. Then they began asking, "Were you me? Were you once me?"

The bowl cracked, the brick crumbled, and a clump of dry, entangled corpses fell to the ground. The child carefully scooped them up. They had regenerated!

She ran to show her mother.

"I'd rather not look," her mother said.

"But, mom, the heads have grown tails, the tails heads!"

With trembling fingers, she began prying them apart in front of her mother's averted eyes. Some turned to ash. Others, however, had miraculously hardened and remained bent like question marks.

"Can they still be used for the Science Fair, Sally?"

"Of course not, mom, but what does it matter?"

The husks lay in her hands, resplendent in their completeness. The child was awestruck. But would the memory of the pencil have remained if they'd lived?

"What difference does it make now?" her mother said.

Perhaps success was all a question of perception. In the back of the child's textbook was a list of famous experiments. One in particular intrigued her. An infant chimpanzee, raised in an environment of horizontal stripes, emerged a year later unable to perceive verticals. A photograph showed the chimp, gleefully devouring bananas, surrounded by her bored brothers and sisters. The caption read, GERTRUDE, WHO NOW RESIDES AT THE BROOKLYN ZOO, LIVES IN A CAGE SHE IS UNABLE TO SEE.

"Mom, I've got to get my hands on a mammal with a bigger cerebral cortex."

A potential subject became available. Otto, the little boy next door, received a kitten for his birthday. The child immediately went to work procuring it. Every morning she harangued Otto with all sorts of arguments; the progress of science, his own humble contribution. But what finally decided the little boy was that he would get to have his name on an experiment for which he did nothing.

He brought over his kitten.

A cardboard box, punctured with air holes, lined with horizontal stripes, sat near the cages of mice and rats.

"Are you sure you know what you're doing?" Otto asked.

"Trust me," the child said.

She grabbed hold of the kitten who, squirming in its last moments of freedom, tried desperately to solicit the saccharine responses it normally evoked in children. It gazed longingly up at the child. Then horizontal stripes appeared before its astonished eyes and the box was slammed shut.

That night, as the child slept soundly for the first time in weeks, her rats and mice popped open their eyes, stumbled out of thick sleep, and became fidgety with nocturnal energy. They gorged themselves on midnight snacks of pellets and literally climbed the walls of their cages. Every now and then a squeaky exercise wheel would burst into motion, whereupon the kitten, alone in its box, ears cocked to the medley of squeaks, would suddenly leap up and down, batting its tail, the only toy it had, between its clumsy paws.

A month later, its huge eyes staring out of its skull, the kitten emerged from the box able to perceive verticals but now completely terrified of horizontals. The child immediately left it on Otto's doorstep.

"Something's wrong! Something's wrong!" the little boy screamed the next morning.

The child peered out the window of her bedroom laboratory.

"You know, I'm not at everyone's beck and call."

"Oh, please," Otto wept hysterically. "Tiger won't come when I'm lying down."

"Then stand up!"

He tried it then and there. It worked!

"You know," Otto said, "the Science Fair is next week."

"Don't you think I'm aware of that?"

"If you use Tiger," he insisted, "I want some of the credit."

"If I use Tiger," the child said, "you can take credit for everything."

She slammed the window and collapsed amid the wreckage of her experiments. Her dyed black mice ambled back and forth like somnambulists. Her moron rats stared out of their dull eyes. She could barely tolerate them. They were attacking their salt lick again, mistaking it for sugar. She burst into tears.

"If only I had had a monkey to work with!"

"Darling," her mother shouted, "Johnny Swat's here. He's come to choose his pick of the rat's litter."

"Pick of the litter?" the child scoffed. "Just let him find one!"

"I'm through, mom. Washed up. Finished."

"What about all our plans for the Science Fair?"

"What would you have me do? Exhibit batches and batches of idiot animals?"

"Maybe you could take up astronomy again?"

"No, thanks! I'm sick of science!"

On the morning of the Science Fair, the child stood glumly in front of the bathroom mirror, brushing out her pigtails until sparks flew.

"I guess you don't want to go to school today, Sally."

"That's putting it mildly, mother."

Suddenly a clump of her electrically charged hair rose up as if by levitation. For a moment, the child was once again bedazzled by science, matter, electricity. Then, raking her hand tragically through her curls, she thought, what difference does it make now?

She lumbered into her bedroom and began dismantling her laboratory. Papers were strewn everywhere, colored graphs torn off the walls.

"We could visit the zoo today," her mother suggested. "See the two-headed snake."

The child rolled her eyes sarcastically.

"Oh, Sally, you used to love things like that! Maybe it will inspire you?"

"Inspire me?" the child said. Looking down at her torn graphs, their optimistic curves crushed underfoot, she exploded into sobs. "What for?"

"There's always next year," her mother said.

The zoo was filled with screeching parrots, riotous monkeys, squealing preschoolers. Her mother wore her blond, helmet-shaped wig. The child had left her clump of pig-tail sticking up. They stood in front of the snake's enclo-sure.

"I'll wait here," her mother said. "I prefer not to see it."

"Oh, mother, it's probably nothing," the child said, yanking her inside.

There were two heads, all right, but only one was for-midable, fully grown, oily and fierce. The other head, a wizened lump, dragged passively behind it. But where else could it go? It hung from its brother's throat like a necktie. If its brother wanted to wrap around a branch, scrutinize the leaves, it had no choice but to look too. It could never close its eyes because snakes have no eyelids. It was forced to stare at everything its sibling found mi-raculous; the leaves, the yellow coils of its own body, the glass enclosure and the people beyond it.

Dumbfounded, the child and her mother stood gap-ing.

The snake began slithering toward them.

Why should such a creature exist, or herself, or her mother for that matter? The child stared at this double-headed monster, at the branching of its forked neck. The snake was now pressed against the glass, its scaly jaws slack, its four black eyes open. It was staring back at them and suddenly, within their depths, the child sensed a glimmer of perpetual amazement, and realized what sci-ence had been trying to tell her all along; that we are all alive despite the tremendous odds of genetics.

Still astounded, she turned to her mother and tried to

explain the whole thing in terms her mother could understand.

"Mom," she began, "isn't it unbelievable that you exist!"

"Yes," her mother said, backing away in horror. "Yes."

SMALL CLAIMS

1

In the days of my childhood, as I look back on them, my love of art seemed as indelible as ink. My mother and I lived all alone in an aluminum trailer at the edge of the desert. She was a silent woman (we later found out she was going deaf), and in the hermetic solitude of my youth—endless sands, my mother's perplexed stare—I was left pretty much to my own devices. Once a month my father, a merchant sailor who later drowned in a hotel bathtub somewhere in Italy, would send me picture post-cards from all the museums of Europe—Breughel, Goya, Munch, a Michelangelo fresco as light as an envelope—with his love scrawled across their backs in wobbly sea letters. I treasured them. Every night, alone in my aluminum bedroom, I'd pore over my collection of master-pieces like a little-leaguer entranced by a pack of baseball cards, dreaming that his name might one day be among them. You see, as far back as I can remember, I wanted to paint my own masterpiece.

My older cousin Isobel, who grew up two trailers away, had already established a small reputation for herself as a neo-expressionist painter in Los Angeles. At age eigh-teen, determined to become an artist myself, I cashed in my father's pension, packed up my postcard collection and followed her to the city. I even rented the studio next door to Isobel's, an elf-sized room with plaster-swaddled pipes. But save for her shrill, intelligent voice filtering through the paper-thin wall between us, I rarely saw or heard from her.

I didn't mind. For the first few months I created, all day and all night, my productivity stunning me. Sometimes I'd envision some poor forest felled and mashed to a pulp to provide the reams of paper that passed under my brush. Even my poverty struck me as romantic. When icy drafts leaked under the windowpanes, I'd wrap myself in old newspapers, like a cubist collage, before getting back to work. I sculpted, drew, gessoed canvases; at night, inspired by my only working light bulb, I'd paint still lifes in boisterous chiaroscuro. Most of the work ended up in the garbage, but if a drawing showed promise, I'd photograph it like a starlet.

One morning, stuffed under my door, I found a crumpled leaflet announcing that the Mary Plank Gallery was having its Annual Emerging Talent Exhibition. An entry form was stapled to the top. I assumed that Isobel had left it. I was ecstatic. Immediately I pinned up all my work, ruminating over what to submit. I paced, squinted, gnawed off a couple of fingernails. Then, for the first time, I scrutinized my work with the cold appraisal of another's eye. Everything looked dreadful. My drawings hung like a cobweb of strokes, the still lifes looked dead, and a little sculpture, the armature on which I'd hung my hopes, suddenly seemed to sag and collapse.

Small claims

For several minutes I tried to calm down, telling myself I could always do more. More? I couldn't even find an original idea! I panicked. I fled from my studio, plopped down on the front stoop and cradled my head in my hands. When the landlady's teenage daughter bounded up the steps, followed by my neighbor Arthur, I ignored them.

"What am I going to do?" I groaned out loud.

"You could always have yourself committed," she suggested, slamming the screen door behind her.

"Oh, don't listen to her," my neighbor said kindly, placing an elderly hand on my shoulder. "Besides, I'm rather a fan of yours. I've even framed one of your drawings."

"Where in all God's name did you get it?"

"From your garbage can."

I burst into tears.

"Why are you crying?"

I told him about the exhibition, my work, the sagging sculpture.

"That's ridiculous," he said.

He scooped me up by my shoulders, escorted me through the entry and unlocked his door. His room was crammed with so many knickknacks it looked like a bazaar. I flopped down on the sofa while he brought me a tepid cup of tea.

"If only I had your talent," he said.

I let my head roll sarcastically to one side.

"What do you know?"

"I used to be a dental technician but since my retire-

45

ment, I've become an artist myself. Right now I'm working on a series of mosaics based on the world's masterpieces."

He offered me a Kleenex into which I blew and blew. Swabbing my eyes, I groped for another until finally, through the veils of tissue, I noticed that he was tiptoeing away.

"And now that you've dropped by," he shouted from the catacombs of a closet, "if it's not too much of an imposition, I wonder if you might give me your opinion of them."

I lowered the Kleenex.

He sallied out of the closet.

I stared aghast.

"This is Leonardo da Vinci's *Last Supper*," he explained, proudly holding up one, done entirely in dried fruit and toothpicks.

The apostles were carved out of apricot slices, and their red robes looked like apple skins. Some of their bodies had oxidized and, jutting out of rotting sleeves, spindly toothpicks pointed to their beloved Christ who gazed heavenward through two shriveled raisins.

For a moment, he beamed over its fruit-laden surface, then carefully set it aside and dragged out another.

"And this one," he said, carrying it out of the closet's shadows, "is my *Mona Lisa* made up entirely of womanly things."

Two buttons with black threads like kewpie doll lashes stared out from a surface of chintz and sequins. Her hair was literally ribbons. And her famous smile, now a row of cracked pearls, glinted before me, their needle holes like gaping cavities.

I rose to leave.

"Please don't go," he said. "I have so many others. Besides, you haven't given me your honest opinion yet."

I couldn't bring myself to say anything. I inched backward toward the door.

"Perhaps you'd like to see something more contemporary?"

He lowered Mona, reeled around, and began rummaging through his closet. A din of banging echoed through the apartment.

"It's not necessary," I said.

"But it's no trouble."

Through the open closet door, I could see his elderly frame stooping painfully on its knees, crawling amid his mosaics.

"You're the first person I've ever shown them to."

I had to get out. I reached for the doorknob, yanking it open.

"One more," he pleaded.

Reluctantly I turned around and there, between his tremulous hands, was the most beautiful thing I'd ever seen. Teeth. Howling configurations of teeth.

"It's Edvard Munch's *The Scream*," he explained, "done entirely in dentures and bridgework."

I quietly shut the door behind me.

"And you haven't shown it to anyone," I said.

2

In the history of art, as I surmised from my postcard collection, old paintings spawn new ones with the Darwinian logic of evolution. A giantess who once roamed the frescoes of Michelangelo will eventually shed her muscular hide and evolve into the goosefleshed lady of a Renoir. Or, under Picasso's brush, a Nigerian death mask suddenly mutates and becomes the cubist portrait of a Parisian matron. If that dandified Spaniard with his pupilless black eyes could pilfer the masks and figurines of all Africa, why, by God, couldn't I snitch one tiny idea from an old man's closet?

I flopped back onto his sofa. We drank pots of tea. I'd never been so thirsty in my life. Then, as politely as I could, I excused myself to go and prepare my portfolio for the exhibition.

"You've changed your mind about the show? I'm so delighted!" Arthur said, adding, "I hope I've been a help."

"You certainly have," I said.

As soon as I got to my studio, I rummaged through my postcard collection, pulled out Edvard Munch's *The Scream* and, carrying pencil, paper and postcard into the bathroom, modeled my own canines in front of the mirror. For a moment, thinking about Arthur, I almost couldn't bring myself to do it. I tapped the rubber end of my pencil guiltily along my teeth. Then, very carefully, I plied its point to the paper and after a few tentative strokes did several very good drawings. One charcoal sketch was particularly spectacular. The sky was a mass of molar-shaped clouds, the river a flood of incisors; in a burst of inspiration, I'd connected the trestles on the bridge of Munch's masterpiece with adolescent braces.

I flopped down on the toilet seat, telling myself it was the best thing I'd ever done. Definitely a minor master-piece. But why minor? It was a masterpiece. Then, glanc-ing into the mirror, I said, "My God in heaven and you're so young!"

I still had a couple of hours before the Mary Plank Gallery closed. I ran to get my portfolio from under the stack of still lifes that only this morning I had wept over. Now even they didn't look so bad. I chose slides repre-senting the best, slipped my drawing on top, gawked at it for a minute or two, raced through the streets of down-town Los Angeles, opened the gallery doors, bumped into a sculpture, apologized, then slunk past a wall of paint-ings and approached the front desk.

The receptionist was filing a set of blood-red nails.

I coughed and, with my voice cracking somewhere in the register of a bat squeal, asked to see the curator.

She sighed without looking up and used the dagger of her emery board to point me toward a glass office. In-side, an elderly gentleman was moving listlessly back and forth, like a fish in an aquarium.

I opened the door. Immediately we scrutinized one another and for a moment, in our mutual hope, we came true for each other like a dream; this decrepit old man with his plastered forelock was transformed into an eccentric curator and I, in my mismatched socks, a flighty gallery dealer. We clasped liquid palms, offered each other a chair. And as the first misconstrued minute limped along in dream time, our futures unraveled flawlessly before us.

Then we pulled out our portfolios.

"You're not a dealer?" he said.

"How humiliating," I said.

And we slumped against opposite walls, staring at each other in abject hatred.

The secretary walked in.

"May I help you?" she asked.

"Yes," the old man said, "I have something to show you."

He reached into the black chasm of his portfolio, pulling out a small box labeled *Pins by Sanford Rupplesberg*.

"I'm sorry," the secretary said, "but we don't allow anything to be tacked up on our walls."

"On your walls?" the old man said. "You've misunderstood me."

He peeled the lid off his box. In stiff, precise rows, like an entomology collection minus the specimens, straight pins were stabbed head-up and labeled.

"You see," he explained, "I've painted all the important events of my life on the heads of these pins."

"You what?" the secretary said.

"I've painted all my important memories in microscopic miniature."

"What on earth possessed you?"

"I don't know," the old man said. "At the time it just seemed so right. I'd very much like the curator to see them."

"So would I," the secretary said.

She tapped on the glass and called over the curator, a spindly young woman with a haystack-like hairdo. The old man proudly explained his art.

"You're joking," the curator said.

"Not at all," the old man said.

He held up his forest of straight pins. Slightly aghast, the curator leaned over them and, for a moment of agricultural oddity, haystack and forest fused.

"They can't be enjoyed by the naked eye but with the help of a microscope."

The old man produced a tiny contraption and pleaded with her to take another look.

"I'm sorry," the curator said.

"I'd very much like to have a show of my pins."

"I'm sorry," the curator said.

"They wouldn't take up much space."

"I'm sorry," the curator said, "but this sort of work has already been done before."

Slowly, a small trembling began to roll through his forest of pins. Jittery tops, weighted with dabs of paint, tilted in havoc. One pin was felled.

"Are you sure?" he asked.

"Absolutely," the curator said. Then she spied a couple of clients through the glass and politely excused herself.

For a moment, I thought the old man might impale himself on his memories.

I asked, "May I take a look?"

"What difference does it make?"

He handed me the magnifying contraption. I bent over its circular lens. For a while, it seemed as if I was peering into a vortex. My vision swirled down the tubular glass. Then, suddenly, the old man's memory snapped into focus. He had painted himself on his knees, head bent over the lap of a woman. She was drawn in the pale colors of death, supine on a velvety surface. Spindly lashes, like the microscopic tenacles of bacteria, spilled out of her lids.

"That's me at my mother's funeral. It might as well be mine. I'm very disillusioned," the old man said. And closing the lid of his box, he cradled his pins to his chest and trudged out the door.

"Now, what can we do for you?" the secretary asked.

I unzipped my portfolio and pulled out the slides of my still lifes.

"I'm sorry," she said, "but our light box isn't working today."

So, cheek to cheek, we held them up to the glaring track lights and peered into their miniature windows.

"Hmmmm. I doubt whether the curator will have time to view these today. Can you leave them with us?"

I was so overjoyed she hadn't just tossed me out that I

babbled, "Oh, that's no problem. I understand completely. Up to your necks in work, eh?"

"Do we have your phone number?"

"It's been disconnected," I explained.

"Your address?"

I rattled it off. Then, looming over her shoulder as she plucked up my slides, I mentioned, "I also have a drawing."

"Well, leave it as well. You should be getting a letter from us soon."

"Please don't rush for my sake. Frankly, I have all the time in the world."

"Until then," she said.

"Until then," I parroted.

3

From the moment I left the gallery, I began mooning for a response. A week went by without an answer. I was condemned to wait in my studio. I didn't dare leave because my mail arrived at sporadic hours. Every day, instead of painting, I'd listen for my postman's footsteps, the jangle of his jailer's keys as he unlocked the metal cell of my mailbox. Then, still in my pajamas, I'd fly down the steps and peer between its cold bars.

Nothing.

One afternoon Mrs. Kribble, the landlady's elderly mother, lumbered down the staircase behind me.

"You're just the person we've been looking for."

On one of her shoulders, like a capsized headdress, perched her parrot, Fredrika.

I politely lied that I was in the middle of working and scurried over to my mail slot.

"I'm sorry," she said, "we didn't mean to disturb you, but with you artists it's so hard to tell."

Something was jammed behind its bars. I wrenched open the door and a stack of bills came toppling out, fluttering around my feet. I almost burst into tears.

"What's wrong?" she asked kindly.

"I'm . . . I'm just so disappointed," I said. "I'm just so discouraged that nothing's working out like I'd planned."

"Fredrika's had her disappointments too," she said sadly.

"Your parrot?"

Hunched over her shoulder in a puff of motley feathers, the creature sat chewing on its own foot. Its head was drooped. Its eyes were closed. But every now and then a scaly lid rolled back and an orange eye stared out at us with otherworldly boredom.

"Parrots live very long lives," Mrs. Kribble explained, "but I'm afraid Fredrika's quite old now. Actually, we're of a comparable age."

"You look much younger," I said politely.

I stooped down and scooped up my bills.

"Thank you," she said.

She placed a wizened hand on my shoulder.

"What concerns me now, what troubles me most, is which one of us will go first."

"Oh, I'm sure it'll be the parrot."

I began thumbing through the bills—gas, electricity, a scarlet notice from the phone company.

"What I'd like to see happen, what I'd like to do for my Fredrika is to figure out a way to have her immortalized."

Suddenly, one of the envelopes caught my eye. I tore open its flap, yanked out the letter and, for a moment, my heart no longer beat, it frollicked in my chest. The gallery had accepted my drawing!

"I'm famous," I stammered.

"Famous?" Mrs. Kribble said. "Famous? Actually, Arthur

suggested that I think along the lines of having you do Fredrika's portrait."

I came out of my daze and stared at the old woman. Hands pressed together, she was looming toward me, the wings of her parrot fiercely spread.

"Well?" she said. "Something to preserve the memory of my Fredrika?"

"Preserve?" I said, turning back to my letter. "I don't know, why don't you have the bird stuffed?"

4

Dear Artist,

We are very happy to announce the inclusion of your *drawing* for our Annual Emerging Talent Exhibition: SEVENTY-FIVE NEO-LOS ANGELE-NOS. All framing costs, additional mailing postage, and unforeseen expenses must be paid by the artist. Welcome aboard.

Cordially,

Mary Plank

Mary Plank, Curator

I must have read and reread that letter a dozen times. I couldn't wait to tell somebody. Oh, I'd already mentioned it to Mrs. Kribble in my own way. Arthur was completely out of the question, under the circumstances. Clutching my letter, I bounded up the staircase to tell Isobel. I was about to pound on her door when I heard voices inside. Obviously a party was going on. I couldn't very well burst in uninvited. I slunk back into my studio. For a while I tried to amuse myself by memorizing my

letter, its envelope, Mary Plank's signature. Then I realized I hadn't a soul in the world to whom I could show it. I collapsed on my bed.

The light had now capsized and the day flowed away, leaving my studio in a spaceless twilight. Corners dissolved and everything appeared to be drenched in gray. The furniture looked like edgeless, formless, luminary lumps. I could make out the craterous hole of my gaping smock sleeve draped over a chair. And all around, jutting out of waterless jars and cans, the bristling mad hair of my brushes seemed to conspire in the dark like Goya's witches. I put my letter away and fell, no, dissolved into sleep.

Suddenly there was a pop, as startling as an explosion. I raised my head. A nail had burst through my wall, nosed about, found nothing to drill into save air, then retreated, leaving a small gap of light. I rubbed the sleep from my eyes. Then another and another burst through, groping around in my airspace before yanking themselves back. I abruptly sat up. For a moment, I didn't know what to do. I simply waited and listened. Explosions would sound, followed by the noses of nails and then more light. Above me, in the darkness, a small constellation was forming. Finally a nail actually connected with a stud and my whole room quaked, turning points of light into shivering beams. Half-asleep, I peered quizzically through the holes as if through the ceiling of the sky.

In the next room Isobel, still holding a hammer, was about to hang up one of her finished canvases to show to a group of local young artists. They stood examining

it behind her. I recognized most of their faces—Tom and Tom, a twin performance team, several up-and-coming expressionist painters and Flow, a glowing neon sculptress who always ignored me—in short, almost everyone I could ever dream of gloating over about my success. So, clearing my throat, I pounded on the wall, shouting, "Isobel, is this going to keep up all night?" Then, very deftly, I added that my opening would be in a couple of days and I didn't want to go with dark circles under my eyes!

A moment later an apologetic Isobel, surrounded by her entourage, appeared at my door. They flopped down on my bed and floor, querying me about my triumph. I scurried over to my refrigerator to see what I could serve: one stone-cold peach, a puckered apple and a branch of withered grapes.

While the artists gobbled down my fruit, Isobel came over, extending her iridescent nails like talons. For a moment, I hoped she might finally take me under her wing. We shook hands.

"I'm very proud of you," she said. "Would you mind if I went with you to your opening?"

"Are you kidding?" I said.

"We can hang out together and, of course, you can introduce me to the curator."

I don't know what possessed me but I raised my hand, entangling two fingers, and said, "We're like this."

The traffic of conversation had changed directions, veering away from me. I quickly guided it back.

I said, "Would anyone like to see my letter?"

A pimply young painter seemed mildly interested.

I read it to him like a proclamation.

I was having a terrific time. In order to give Isobel and me a little more in common, I said, "What a crazy building we live in."

"It sure is," Isobel said. "Between Mrs. Kribble and her parrot, you'd think we were living in an asylum."

I told her about the portrait commission and everybody laughed uproariously.

"And what about that nut who lives downstairs," the pimply boy chirped up. "I heard he was making mosaics!"

The room burst into crackling laughter. Isobel's wall-eyes rolled back. Flow, the sophisticated neon sculptress, doubled over slapping her knees like a farmer's wife. But I remained perfectly still, feeling extremely faint.

"Has anybody seen them?" I asked.

They shook their heads no.

"Nobody's seen them," I said.

And just as their laughter died down, my shrill and nervous laughter rose.

5

On the morning of my opening, dark circles did appear under my eyes, but not from lack of sleep. They were the result of my jittery hand trying to improvise some mascara with a brush of acrylic black paint. I was a little worried that my eyelashes might fall out. I didn't have any money left to buy proper makeup: at Mary Plank's suggestion, I'd spent the last of it on a walnut wood frame. She just happened to have one in her adjacent frame shop.

Isobel was standing in the doorway. "You'd better hurry up!"

Arranging my curls in the mirror, I grabbed a can of hair spray and squeezed the trigger, whereupon a bubble, the last of its gluey contents, inflated and burst. I finished up with a blast of fixative instead.

It was a beautiful day. A flock of white seagulls was scribbled across the sky and above them pink clouds of all sizes and shapes rolled by. We drove in Isobel's convertible, the wind roaring around us. Whenever the sun popped out, glass skyscrapers reflected the scene like vertical lakes. We parked in front of the gallery. Immediately I checked my hair in the rear-view mirror.

"You look fine," Isobel insisted. She dragged me out of the car and opened the gallery doors.

The room was teeming with people. I stopped for a moment to bask in the light of attention I assumed would flood over me. But when I wedged my way up to the curator, she only shook my hand limply a couple of times and let it drop.

Most of the people were drinking. Others swarmed around the hors d'oeuvres. When a fresh platter arrived, squadrons of fingers landed like flies on the cheese. And all around, clinging to the walls, the jilted artwork hung ignored. Only the exhibiting artists stood next to their paintings.

"Whatever you do," Isobel advised, "don't stand next to your drawing. It frightens potential buyers away."

So I slouched against every wall but the one on which my drawing hung. I wasn't quite sure what to do. A young painter, looking as nervous as I, escorted an elderly woman through the turmoil.

"Just a little farther, mother."

He cupped her elbow and guided her over to a painting.

"It's mine," he stammered softly.

"Yours?" the old woman said.

"Yes, mother, my very first exhibition."

"Help me on with my glasses!"

Two bottle-thick lenses were slipped on her nose.

"And this one is yours?"

"Yes, mother, yes."

He pointed to the name plate. *Untitled* by Phillip Swann.
Proudly, she began scanning his painting.

"I can't seem to make anything out," she confided awkwardly. "Perhaps, son, it's only me."

"Pardon me, Mrs. Swann," I chirped in, finally mingling, "your son's painting is an abstraction."

"An abstraction?" the old woman said, scrutinizing the maze of paint. "I always knew he'd take the easy way out."

Isobel was chattering with a group of artists from a rival gallery. They bantered back and forth while I stood hovering around the edge, hoping to be noticed. Every now and then I'd blurt out some bitter remark, trying to be funny. Across the gallery two matrons appeared, their necks swiveling in ropes of jewels. Under the track lights, sequins ignited along the flanks of their gowns.

"See those two women," Isobel said. "I think they're on the verge of buying."

Everybody turned. From painting to drawing, the matrons revolved around the room. Suddenly, one of their shaved and repainted eyebrows rose in awe. Then a finger, sluggish from the weight of its diamond, drifted upward and pointed to my drawing!

I rose majestically to the moment.

"Oh, please pardon me," I said, and wedged my way past their slack jaws, their incredulous eyes.

The matrons stood transfixed in front of my sketch.

"I don't know," the first one said.

"But I think it looks lovely," the second one argued.

On tiptoe I peered between their matching hairdos. In the reflective glass frame, I imagined I saw their eyes become hypnotically glazed.

"Well, you're the one with taste," the first one sighed.

She popped open the gold latch of her purse. My eyes were riveted to her hand as it dipped inside and, for a moment, the whole gallery dissolved and I was groping my way along with her fingers through unfathomable trinkets. We emerged with a billfold.

Then the most horrible transformation took place; the billfold grew teeth and metamorphosed into a comb before my eyes. They began combing their ridiculous new hairdos in my reflective glass frame. Then their faces veered away and I stood staring at my own, black acrylic tears winding down my cheeks.

6

Imagine an onslaught of tears absorbing everything they pass, so that the world seems veiled forever in their waters. That is what I saw as I fled the gallery: boulevards of sopping pedestrians, drenched cars, doused trees. I must have wandered about for hours, turning blurry corners, dodging through smears of traffic. Every now and then I sat down on a bench to dry my eyes with my fingers. Around dusk I finally returned home. Arthur was peeking out his door. As soon as he saw me, he swept off his glasses and playfully rolled his eyes heavenward.

"Will she . . . will she still talk to us mortals?"

He winked, he clasped his hands together, he drew me into his apartment.

"Mrs. Kribble told me about your big success. How did it go?"

I dangled my acrylic-stained fingers in front of him.

"The curator barely shook my hand."

He awkwardly pressed them to him, hunched over, and examined them with his myopic eyes. Then, very gently, he wiped off a glob or two of paint.

"There," he said, returning them to me, "there, there."

I suddenly couldn't support my waterlogged head another minute. I laid it against his chest. The warmth of his body enveloped me and, for a moment, we simply stood there, Arthur at rigid attention, me like a wet towel laid against the ribbing of a heater. Once I saw his tremulous hands move to embrace me, falter, stop. I stepped back. Then I quietly kissed him, stunning us both.

"You'd better go now," he said.

I didn't say anything. Above his bed hung the drawing of mine he'd found in the garbage and framed. I looked at it and, for the first time in my life, there seemed nothing so unremarkable as art.

I decided to accept the commission to paint the parrot.

Isobel was home. Lights from her studio poured through the nail holes. I peered through, about to announce my decision, when I noticed she was working. She approached a canvas as if stalking it from afar, camouflaged in a thicket of brushes. They jutted out of every pocket, some were clenched between her teeth. And the used ones, now oozing colors, grew in her fist until they became as thick as bouquets.

Once she'd gotten rolling, her whole room trembled. Jars spilled, cans overturned and her brushes, dropping here and there, crashed to the floor, falling around her feet like slaves.

Suddenly she stopped and carried the canvas over to my wall. My studio went black. I had to crawl under my bed where a gap of light still showed. I could barely breathe. When my ribs expanded, wads of dust clogged my nose. I carefully fit an eye to the starry nail hole.

Isobel was now sprawled on an overstuffed chair. I knew

she couldn't see me but I winced nevertheless. From my perspective, her feet appeared gargantuan, the trunk of her body monstrously foreshortened. She was gazing in rapture at the painting above me. Even behind the wall I could sense her excitement. She'd gulp, sigh, and luxuriously stroke an earlobe. Once her jaw dropped open in awe.

For a while I watched her, stunned by her unabashed pride. Then I was weeping soundlessly in the dark.

7

The next morning I banged on our wall. "Isobel," I said, "I suppose I've got to accept the old hag's offer to let me paint her chicken now."

"Don't be a lunatic," Isobel said, "you still have a couple of weeks before the show comes down. Besides, if you don't sell your drawing, you can always do the insurance number."

"The what?"

"The insurance number. My God, you are naive."

A moment later she appeared in my doorway, wagging her head in disbelief. Then, features working, her walleyes drifting, she painted me a scene of unbelievable simplicity. I would take out a policy on my drawing, accidentally damage it on the way home from the gallery, then file a small claim.

I said, "Isobel, you don't understand, that's my first exhibited piece."

"It's up to you."

From her back pocket, she pulled out a newspaper.

"A review of my show?"

"Not exactly," Isobel said.

I grabbed the newspaper. I flipped it open to the art section.

"Sanford Rupplesberg? I can't believe this," I said.

Blown up in grainy circular reproductions, Sanford's infinitesimal memories were plastered across the page. Sanford himself was photographed underneath, dressed in an ascot and flinching gallantly under the frozen backslaps of two museum curators. The caption read, *Pricked by Inspiration Local Watchmaker Takes Artworld by Storm.* I skimmed over the laudatory review and read a closing quote by Sanford. "I guess I always knew my pins would be a smash."

I said, "Isobel, could you suggest an insurance company."

Two weeks later when my drawing hadn't sold, I made all the necessary arrangements with her insurance agency. They sent me a policy while I, at Isobel's suggestion, kept promising my check was in the mail.

I couldn't quite believe what I'd stooped to.

On the evening before my show came down, I took out my postcard collection and tried to conjure up images of my childhood. I envisioned my aluminum bedroom, my former self—flannel pajamas, budding breasts, pigtails, translucent ears—gawking for hours over those masterpieces all flooded in silver light. Then I looked at myself in the mirror. Do humans shed their souls from time to time the way reptiles shed skins?

The next morning I picked up my drawing at the gallery, checked to make sure Arthur wasn't home, carried it tenderly to the top of the staircase and, with Isobel's help, shoved it over the banister. For a moment my drawing seemed to take flight, hovering gracefully over the gully of steps as in a dream. Next it collided with the landlady's light fixture and, as if rudely slapped awake, plummeted downward. It crashed against a step with a horrifying echo, shattering glass and wood, turned several drunken cartwheels and impaled itself on my landlady's umbrella. This all lasted two seconds. Then I was miraculously at its side, cradling it in my lap. Shards of glass were everywhere and I was drenched in charcoal.

Saucer-eyed neighbors stood gap-mouthed in their doorways.

"Terrific," Isobel whispered. "You've got witnesses."

"What the hell is going on here?" the landlady yelled, opening her screen door. Behind it the gauzy outline of her daughter's face pressed against the wires.

I scooped up the remains of my drawing. A hunk of frame hung limply, drooping in my arms like a broken limb. Then, ignoring my landlady's babbling, I carried it gently upstairs past all the kind funerary expressions of my neighbors.

As soon as I got to my studio, I began washing the charcoal off my hands. I scoured up to my elbows and used a pushpin to clean under my fingernails. A stain of raven black coal lingered on the bottom of the sink. I scrubbed that away with my toothbrush. Then, pocketing my insurance policy, I opened the door and took one last look at my drawing. It was heaped on the floor where I'd dropped it, askew, shattered, unrecognizable.

I climbed down the steps to use the pay phone. The

landlady's daughter was sweeping up my mess. I stepped over her broom, tossed a dime into the slot and dialed the insurance agency.

"There's been an accident," I said.

"Just a moment, let me put you on hold."

For several minutes, a Polish wedding polka played. Then another voice, nasal and fatigued, said, "Yeah?"

"I'd like to report a small claim."

"Okay, report."

In great detail I described my drawing, its fall, the remnants of things it had become. "I have witnesses," I added.

"Swell."

"Sir?"

"Your policy number."

I read out the numbers, carefully enunciating each one. For the letters, I used the military code, rattling them off like a classroom roster—"Charlie, Charlie, Adam, Mary."

"And the amount of your claim."

I checked to make sure the landlady's daughter wasn't listening.

"Four hundred dollars," I whispered.

"May we assume that's over and above the deductible?"

"Pardon me, sir?"

"I said," the voice said, "may we assume that's over and above the deductible. Check your policy, please."

I checked my policy, groping my way through the jungle of legal language, plowing through a thicket of paragraphs until I stumbled onto the last page, where, hidden in a camouflage of italics, I read, *$500.00 deductible.*

I steadied myself on my feet. I tried to calm myself. I gulped down several glasses of air. The telephone receiver had plummeted from my hands, and out of its earpiece I heard a faint voice, like the drone of an insect, calling to me. I silenced it by banging the receiver down. Then I went up to strangle Isobel.

She wasn't there. I stormed in anyhow, determined to ransack her studio, to destroy something—a canvas, a drawing, a gouache. And then I saw it. It was a small painting adrift on her wall amid the punctures of her nail holes, and it was beautiful. It was a painting of a toilet bowl, no more, no less. A nacreous white bowl like a porcelain globe with whirlwinds of water lapping at its sides. She'd painted it in full flush. But there was something about the light. It seemed to radiate from within, a quicksilver light pouring outward from the vortex of the bowl. And in that centrifuge of light and water, half-decomposed and drowning, she'd painted a lone cigarette butt, the loneliest thing I'd ever seen. For a moment, I shrank back from the sheer velocity of its beauty. Then I crept forward determined to smash it.

But I just couldn't do it. Standing there, under its awesome beauty, my anger drained out of me. I crumpled up my insurance policy.

"Sink or swim, fool," I said to myself, "but don't ruin everything."

8

The next morning I knocked on the old woman's door and finally accepted the parrot commission.

"Fredrika will be so delighted that you've changed your mind."

On top of the television antenna, Fredrika slept, hunched over scaly legs. Her beak was folded under the pagoda points of her wings. Her tail drooped. Along the crest of her exposed breast bone, a patch of bird skin bristled and leapt with bird heartbeats. Then, slowly, the glassy pins of her feathers prickled, a scaly lid rolled back and, in a puff of color, Fredrika was awake. Her orange eye immediately telescoped my whereabouts. Her giant beak stretched open. Still clinging to the antenna with her gargoyle feet, her wings fanned open and she began flying in place.

Mrs. Kribble sat down next to me.

"Fredrika," she cooed, "Fredrika."

A rainbow blur streaked across my vision, splashing onto her lap. Immediately they began to preen each other. The bird chewed tenderly on a loose hair, a row of buttons, her pendulous breasts. Mrs. Kribble dug methodi-

73

cally through the animal's plumage—plucking out lice, I guess.

"Don't you think my Fredrika will make a good subject?"

I cautiously studied the bird. Its orange eye glared at me.

"Well?" Mrs. Kribble said, "well?"

Slowly those lethal jaws began to stretch open, wider and wider as though they'd become unhinged. For a moment, the creature was all throat, a black abyss dramatically framed in feathers. Then a gray tongue as long as a finger unfurled, and I realized the animal was only yawning.

"Do you have any photographs?" I asked politely.

"I'm sorry, young woman, but I don't believe in portraiture from photographs. In my humble opinion, it's cheating."

"I meant," I said insanely, "for my wallet."

But Mrs. Kribble ignored me. She turned to Fredrika.

"Is this what you want?" she queried the bird. "Is this what you want, little darling?" Then she dragged a fingernail across the bird's skull, and its feathers fanned, an orange eye rolled back in rapture.

"May I have the bird's cage now?"

"I'm sorry, but Fredrika suffers from claustrophobia. She can ride up to your studio on your shoulder."

An ancient finger scooped under the creature's claws and placed the animal on my shoulder. It immediately climbed up onto my head.

"Look at that," Mrs. Kribble said.

I had my eyes closed.

"Fredrika likes you."

"I certainly hope so," I said. And listening to the patter of claws on the ceiling of my skull, I tactfully inquired about my money.

"I'm a fair woman, but I certainly won't pay for a painting I haven't yet seen."

"You're joking."

"Absolutely not."

For a while we bickered back and forth. Finally, with a great sigh of reluctance, Mrs. Kribble agreed on a third down.

"I am awfully anxious to see how you'll capture my Fredrika," she said.

"So am I."

I stood up, plumage and all.

She handed me the parrot's food, toys, and water bowl.

"This is my Fredrika's first time away from home. I hope you'll take good care of her."

"Of course," I said.

As soon as I got to my studio, I scratched the creature out of my hair. She plummeted to the floor. Then, arming myself with a paint brush, I herded her into a corner.

9

My studio became an aviary of Fredrikas. The bird was everywhere. She wouldn't stand still. While I arranged a palette of parrot colors—tropical pinks, azure blues, banana yellows—the squawking creature flew this way and that. When she wasn't flying, she hobbled underfoot, pecking at my toes. Sometimes she'd perch on my easel top, screeching phrases she'd picked up from her mistress.

"Is the gas off!" "Did I shut the lights!"

A waterfall of her molting feathers landed on everything. I didn't know where to begin. In desperation I picked up a brush and splashed on tropical colors. But the blues turned sullen, the yellows whined, the pinks resented their placement. And somewhere on top, where I'd sketched out her eye, a swelling blob of belligerent orange kept bursting through its borders, leaking over everything.

The creature was flapping overhead.

"Stand still!" I screamed.

Then I walloped the bird with my brush handle. She bit off a piece, somersaulted, and dangled by her gargoyle feet.

"Oh God, I quit, I quit!" I cried in frustration.

From the dark corner of my studio where the bird had now fluttered, she let out an ear-throbbing whistle. Then, in a voice indisputably my own but pitched high up into the octaves of a jungle cry, she screeched, "I quit! I quit!"

"Isobel," I said, pounding on the wall, "I can't paint this hyperkinetic creature. She simply won't stand still."

"Then use a photograph," Isobel suggested.

"I'm not allowed. In the old hag's humble opinion portraiture from photographs is cheating."

"Good God," Isobel said. "Perhaps you could have your creature anesthetized."

"And how would I do that?"

"Just slip it a Quaalude."

"Isobel," I said, "that would be complete lunacy."

I turned back to the creature. Wings drawn back, beak ajar, she was hissing on the floor.

"And where in all God's name could I possibly buy some Quaaludes?"

"From the landlady's daughter."

A couple of minutes later, I was ringing my landlady's doorbell.

"Oh, hi, Mrs. Markman. Is Judy home?"

Judy sauntered over to the door. I nudged her outside.

"There's a rumor you make certain pharmaceutical arrangements," I whispered.

"Huh?"

"I'd like to purchase a couple of Quaaludes."

"Oh, 'ludes. Yeah, sure. They're in my locker at school. You'll have to drive me."

"I don't own a car."

"You mean I have to use my bicycle?"

"Yeah, Judy, that's what you get the big bucks for."

An hour later, all flushed and panting, my little dealer pedaled up to me and, in the shade of the building, we concluded our transaction. I immediately headed back up to my studio.

"Does Fredrika want a peanut?" I queried.

Her lethal jaws stretched open with a screech.

"Wonderful!" I said.

I popped a Quaalude into my palm and held it up to her perch. An orange eye immediately inspected it.

"Go ahead," I said.

Bobbing in a blur of feathers and claws, she swooped up the pill in her colossal beak, cracking it to smithereens. I downed the other Quaalude, and within no time we were on the best of terms.

I said, "Hey, Freddie, we've got to get to work."

She was on my lap and we were cracking peanuts together. The whole studio seemed vaguely afloat, shafts of daylight oddly askew. Patches of it rose like steam. I stood up while Fredrika slithered to the floor. I actually had to carry the reeling creature to her perch. Then, while I arranged my brushes and palette, she puffed up her plumage and a moment later, I was truly painting.

A single line captured the drama of flight, a smeared blotch the agony of motion. Colors ran willy-nilly down the canvas. A few scratches connected and Fredrika took shape. I used metallic gold for her beak. I painted beaks everywhere. And for that icy tongue, I splashed on gunmetal blue. Then, in a burst of inspiration, I laid the painting flat and chased Fredrika across it. We were both slightly woozy. I finished up by gluing her toys to the canvas.

I said, "My God, Fredrika, I think I've done it!"

I turned to the creature. I wanted to show her the work, the possibility of my having painted a masterpiece. But Fredrika wasn't looking too well. Her colossal beak was hanging open like a toothless mouth. The oily quills of her feathers showed and underneath, her reptilian skin had broken out in goosebumps. I ran over to the bird. Down fluttered from her tail. She was teetering over her food dish where once-terrified flies now landed in squadrons.

I banged on the wall.

I said, "Isobel, are you there?"

"I'm sleeping!"

"Oh God, Isobel, the bird looks half dead."

"Then do a still life!"

That evening I nursed the bird as best I could. I fed her watered-down milk through an eyedropper. If a scaly lid rolled shut, I'd urge her to her feet, forcing her to walk. Sometimes I'd let her nest on my knees, astonished by the delicacy of her weight. Under her plumage was a tiny corset of ribs against which I could feel her heart thump weakly. Around dawn we both finally fell asleep, me on a chair, she on my lap. One claw, like the shriveled hand of an infant, grasped my fingers.

I awoke hours later. In the morning light, jaws agape, Fredrika rattled when she breathed, the thin parchment of her beak glowing eerily from within.

"Isobel," I called out, "please come. I don't think the bird's looking any better." I gently unpried her claws and scooped her off my lap.

Isobel was standing in the door. "You're right," she said, "the bird does look like she's on her last claw."

"What am I going to do?"

"I suppose you should go tell Mrs. Kribble."

"And what am I supposed to tell her?"

With her iridescent nails, Isobel examined the bird. I stood hovering in the background. Then, almost clinically, she pried open one of Fredrika's lids. An orange eye, glazed and oscillating in its socket, stopped, raked over our faces, then closed.

"Well," Isobel said, "I certainly wouldn't tell her the truth."

10

"My Fredrika? *Ach Gott!*"

Mrs. Kribble slumped against her door and began weeping.

"I'm so sorry," I said. "I don't know what happened."

"Oh, please," she sobbed. "Fredrika is old. It's just that I don't seem to know what to do right now. Would you help us?"

"Of course," I said.

"Can she be moved?"

"She's not in any pain. At least we can be grateful for that."

"Are you sure?"

"Trust me," I said, "the bird doesn't feel a thing."

"May I go to her now?"

"Of course."

But the old woman didn't move. She stood quivering in her doorway, clutching a breast. "I just . . . I just can't bear for my Fredrika to see me like this."

Tenderly, I cupped her elbow and embraced those heaving shoulders. I said, "Really, you look fine."

"I do?"

Tears, confused in a maze of wrinkles, ran down her cheeks. I pulled out a paint rag and dabbed them away.

"My gloves!" she said suddenly.

I helped her on with her gloves.

"What a foolish old woman I am," she said, staring aghast at her hands.

By the time we got upstairs, Isobel had found an old butcher's block to use as a stretcher. Fredrika was lying across it like a game hen. Mrs. Kribble rushed to her side.

"It's me," she stammered softly, scooping up the creature's head and plying her lips to its gaping jaw, "I'm here, Fredrika."

Her flesh-colored gloves stroked the width and breadth of the bird's back. Then she noticed Fredrika's paint bespattered feet.

"Oh my God," she said, "what's happened to my Fredrika's claws?"

I calmly mentioned the technique with which the parrot had participated in her own portrait. Then I turned the canvas to her bereaved eyes and, like a pathologist unable to stop himself from rattling off to a widow all the bizarre details of her husband's death, I proudly explained my art.

"Not bad," Isobel said.

"*Ach Gott,*" Mrs. Kribble said, "that's not my Fredrika!"

She turned back to the bird and, with a burst of uncanny strength, hoisted up the butcher's block.

"Would you girls please call my veterinarian and tell him we're on our way?"

Then, carefully balancing Fredrika on that slab of wood, she fled out the door.

11

The bird in question, a forty-year-old macaw, entered my facility with a slow pulse, a clammy skin texture and extreme dilation of the pupils. By a simple examination, I was able to determine that the parrot had been drugged," the veterinarian testified.

We were all sitting in Small Claims Court. I was in the defendant's chair. Isobel and Arthur had accompanied me for moral support. Mrs. Kribble had brought her daughter, the landlady, and the landlady's daughter Judy to testify. She was suing me for Fredrika's medical expenses while I, at Isobel's suggestion, was counter-suing for the remainder of the portrait commission.

"And what procedures did you take?" the judge asked the veterinarian.

"At the time, the animal was in no immediate danger. Obviously, the drug had been administered—"

"I object!" I said.

"There are no objections in Small Claims Court. Proceed, Doctor."

"I was only going to say that the drug had been taken several hours prior to the bird's arrival and my procedure was one of simple observation."

Small claims

"And how is the animal now?" the judge asked.

"Satisfactory," the veterinarian said.

"Young woman," the judge said, turning to me, "do you know how the parrot was drugged?"

"I have no idea," I said. "The creature was everywhere, chewing on everything. The old woman wouldn't let me have its cage. Perhaps it found an aspirin somewhere, or an allergy pill?"

"Is this possible?" the judge asked the veterinarian.

"Parrots are extremely curious creatures and they do have a tendency to chew. Although I seriously doubt whether the parrot I examined was suffering from the effects of either an antihistamine or an aspirin."

"Were you able to determine exactly what drug had been taken?"

"At the time, testing for the exact drug seemed like an unnecessary expense. As I've said, the animal was out of danger."

"Thank you, Doctor. You may step down."

"May I say something? May I speak now?" Mrs. Kribble said. She raised her hand like a schoolgirl.

"Of course," the judge said. He benevolently signaled the bailiff to help Mrs. Kribble to her feet. She grasped the official's sleeve and, puffing, shakily hoisted herself up. Then she produced a cane I'd never seen before and hobbled toward the bench.

"As you can see, Your Honor, I'm an old woman, obviously under a doctor's care. In my home alone, I keep maybe twenty or thirty different kinds of pills. I keep them uncapped because I suffer from arthritis of the hands."

She showed the judge her gnarled fingers.

"My granddaughter, Judy Markman, is here today to testify to this."

A cold rivulet of sweat rolled down my neck.

Judy's anxious young face, looking more terrified than my own, arose amid the sea of onlookers.

"I uncap them for her myself," she said, then promptly sat down.

"Thank you, Judy. As you can see," the old woman continued, "the opportunity for Fredrika to get into pills is more than ample at home. But"—and she wielded her cane like a weapon—"my Fredrika would never, never do such a thing unless she was forced! I've taken a picture of my pills. I'd like to place them in evidence now, Your Honor."

A polaroid snapshot of vials of multicolored capsules was picked up by the bailiff.

"This is lunacy," I said.

"We'll get to your side in a moment, young lady."

"Judge," Mrs. Kribble said, planting herself at the foot of his bench, "this whole experience has been more than trying for me." She swept off her glasses and dabbed her eyes with a rumpled handkerchief. "Fredrika is all I have. I just want that stated for the records."

"I will certainly take that into consideration."

Signaling for the bailiff, Mrs. Kribble draped herself onto one of his arms and hobbled back to her chair, the tip of her cane dragging loudly behind her.

Then I raised my right hand and the bailiff swore me in.

"State your name and profession."

"I'm a painter," I said.

"House?" the judge asked.

"Artist."

"Ha!" Mrs. Kribble said.

A titter or two broke out among the onlookers.

The gavel reverberated through the courtroom.

"I'm beginning to lose my patience," the judge said. Then, lowering his head, bald and shiny above his black robes, he began thumbing through a stack of official papers.

"In your affidavit," the judge began, reading in a monotone, "you state that you were commissioned by the plaintiff, Mrs. Heinrich Kribble, to paint a portrait of her parrot."

"Yes, Your Honor."

"And that the work, a thirty-six-inch by forty-eight-inch acrylic painting, was completed in good faith and to the best of your ability."

"Absolutely, sir."

"But as of this hearing you have not been paid the balance due you."

"That is correct, Judge."

"Bailiff, could the painting in question please be brought up to the bench."

"Sir!" I said.

"Yes?"

"It looks better at a distance."

"Bailiff, place the painting anywhere the defendant wants it."

I pointed out a clean white wall above an unused jury box. The bailiff grudgingly obeyed. When the painting's plastic tarp was removed, a slight murmuring like a distant rumbling of thunder rolled across the onlookers.

"May we proceed *now?*" the judge asked.

"Of course, Your Honor."

"Is there anything you want to add to your affidavit?"

"I only want to express my deepest sympathy over the parrot's accidental illness. As far as the work goes, I hope my painting speaks for itself."

"Mrs. Kribble, why hasn't this young woman been paid?"

"I'm sorry, Your Honor, but I can't be expected to pay for that *thing.*"

She took out an Audubon Society book.

"This is what *I* had in mind, sir."

The judge turned to me. "Young lady, did you know you weren't supposed to do a cubist painting?"

"Your Honor," I explained, "it's not a cubist painting."

"Nevertheless," the judge continued, "were you informed that the plaintiff didn't want a piece of modern art?"

"Sir, it's not called modern art anymore."

"Then what would you like us to call it!"

"Neo-expressionism or post-minimalism, sir."

"She never called it that before!" Mrs. Kribble blurted out.

"Please!" the judge said. Then he turned back to me. "Young lady, are the parrot's toys adhered permanently to the canvas?"

"Yes, Your Honor."

"And I suppose those gold triangles are meant to represent the beak?"

"Yes, Your Honor."

"May I ask what those blue swirls are?"

"The parrot's tongue, sir."

"That's not my Fredrika!"

"Is there a photograph of the bird in evidence?" the judge asked.

"Yes," the bailiff said.

"May I see it, please."

Another glossy snapshot was whisked up to the bench.

"Your Honor," I whispered, "may I see you in private?"

"Absolutely not. This is a Small Claims proceeding."

With several slipshod glances, he compared the polaroid to my painting.

"Sir, that photograph is irrelevant. It has nothing to do with contemporary art! Or any art for that matter!"

Mrs. Kribble's hand popped up.

"Yes?"

"May I? May I read the court something?" She took out a large tattered dictionary embossed with the year of its origin—1928. "Art," she read in a crackling voice, "the ability to arrange and re-create natural things by human *skills*. Need I say more?"

"No, Mrs. Kribble, I believe that's sufficient. Will both parties please rise."

Mrs. Kribble rose spryly to her feet, but I remained where I was. I turned to Isobel and Arthur. Isobel was nowhere in sight but Arthur was gazing in rapture at my painting.

"Although it is not the duty of this court to pass judgment on aesthetics," the judge said, "I find myself tempted to rule in favor of the plaintiff. A living creature's health must take precedence over the merits of art. Young lady, before I officially close these proceedings, is there anything you wish to add?"

I stood up. I was practically in tears. I stared at the judge's expressionless face, the bailiff's stifled yawn, Mrs. Kribble's gloating eyes. Then I looked at my painting. Across the sterile room, under the court's harsh light, a multitude of Fredrikas flapped and clawed, each hue appearing more radiant until, like a flock of colors, I could see the whole spectacle of her species in pigment. And the parrot's toys, glued over everything, cast a jungle of wild shadows. It suddenly didn't matter if it was a masterpiece or not; it was beautiful.

"Will the defendant please address herself to this bench!"

I couldn't take my eyes off my own painting.

I said, "Don't any of you understand? It's the best thing I've ever done."

Then the gavel slammed and my case was closed.

MONEY

Part One: Savings

1

As far back as I can remember, I wanted to have my picture taken over the landscape of New York, to cast my shadow from some unfathomable height; and later, to be able to hold in my hand a replica of the exact moment I metamorphosed from country bumpkin to city girl. . . .

With my meager life savings, I arrived in Manhattan.

The practical thing was to find a room, which I did, and a job, which I didn't. As long as I had money in my pockets I felt I could put off the inevitable; I watched with pity as a tide of young women were swallowed up every morning by anonymous buildings. I, like every fool before me, was convinced my destiny was special. I was sixteen, I had my money, scraped together by part-time jobs waitressing with my mother, and an old tour book, bequeathed to me by an old aunt who had died of tuberculosis somewhere in the city. I'm said to have resembled her.

For the first few days I was extraordinarily lonely. I took a tour suggested by little red footprints in my tour book, but after that I rarely ventured out. I didn't know where to go. The city disoriented me. I ate in a local cafeteria, sat in a local park and spent my evenings locked in my room, leafing through the tour book or counting up my money. I became a little obsessed with counting my money—ten, twenty, sometimes thirty times a night. If the neighbors bickered or a toilet flushed, I'd make myself start over at the beginning. Most of my money was in traveler's checks but I still had a small wad of bills. One night, feeling particularly lonesome, I lined them up end to end to see how far they'd extend. I even made a tower out of my coins.

Perhaps I'd still be in that room, an ancient miser crippled over my coins, if I'd never met Yvette. After a week of eating, sitting and counting, my daily routine began to take on the drudgery of a job. I resented not being paid. My room gave me claustrophobia. My savings were dwindling fast. So one morning, before plopping down on the park bench I'd occupied for a week, I decided to buy myself the want ads. A row of newspaper machines was chained to the trunk of a tree. An old man, bent over his cane, was reading their various headlines.

"Sir," I said, "could you suggest a paper with a good classified section?"

He rapped on the legs of a machine with the tip of his cane.

"Thank you," I said. I pulled out my change. Then I turned back to him, adding, "Would you like one?" It was morning, the sun was streaming through the trees and this was the first conversation I'd had in a week. I suddenly felt very benevolent. I said, "Let me get you a paper, sir. It's on me."

I tossed my change into the slot.

"I don't think so," the old man said.

"Oh, it's no problem. I've already paid."

"No," the old man said, "I don't think so."

"There's nothing to think about. I'll just take two."

I opened the jaws of the machine.

"Please," the old man said.

"It's nothing," I insisted, "nothing at all." From between the jaws I removed two papers, slamming the window shut. I said charmingly, "Oops, ha, it's too late now." Then I held the papers up, saying, "Take one!"

"Please!" the old man said. With stiff dignified movements he arranged himself around the handle of his cane. His small breast rose prominently in his vest. An aged hand swept a lock of hair into a rigid gleaming part.

I kept the papers extended, insisting, "Go ahead and take one, sir!"

"Please!" the old man said, "you're humiliating me."

"I'm what?" I said. I was stunned. A leaf of the papers stirred in the breeze, rippling against my wrists. I scratched them feverishly. I said, "I'm—"

But the old man had turned away. On bended legs he teetered down a pathway, thrusting his cane before him. A row of elderly women were seated on the park bench across from me. I was too embarrassed to lower my papers. I pretended to read them at arm's length. Suddenly I felt a tap on my shoulder. I turned in a windmill of papers, arms and me. Standing in the middle of the path was a young woman with an outstretched hand.

"I'll take it," she said.

And before I could lower my arms she reached out and selected the least smeared of my papers.

"God, this is just terrific," she said, peeling off the news section and placing it over the slabs of my bench. Then she sat down on top of it.

I was still staring so she pointed to my spot beside her on the bench.

"Take a seat," she said.

I did, carefully maneuvering myself out of the view of the elderly women. I opened my paper and barricaded myself behind the columns of the want ads—drapery sales, drapery installer, drapery seamstress, dry cleaner presser, dry cleaner spotter, counter clerk, cleaning spotter, dry finisher.

"Are you looking for a job?" she asked.

"Why, yes," I said anxiously.

"Professional?"

"Anything."

"Uh," she said.

Trainee, typist, tech, lab, punch, key, elevator operator, executive typist, insurance typist, medical transcriber, casualty rating file clerk—suddenly, I envisioned those anonymous buildings and saw myself washed into them every morning with the tide of women. I couldn't prod my pencil to circle anything. I turned the pages miserably.

"Hey," she said, "take a look at this."

Over the columns of my paper, I peered across to hers. It was spread open to the bride's section. The sun was glaring and I carried a sort of optical replica of the want

SMALL CLAIMS

ads before my eyes. For a moment I scanned it, insanely searching for a job amidst the congratulatory columns.

"Not there," she said, pointing, "here."

Under the tip of her finger was a small photograph of a young bride. It paled next to the striking red polish of her nail.

"Well?" she said, "well?"

I couldn't see anything abnormal. The bride had her fingers interlocked, her elbows akimbo.

"Take a closer look," she insisted.

The edge of her gown was furbelows. A pleat of lace grazed her throat.

"What am I looking for?"

"The veil," she said, "look under the veil."

Spilling out of a garland, a sheath of finery hid the bride's face. I scrutinized the mysterious shadows beneath it, assuming that the print had smeared.

"Eyeglasses," she said, "she's got on eyeglasses."

Suddenly, those shadows of mysterious dots arranged themselves into lenses. Posing for her wedding picture, the little bride, all bedecked, peered out from behind the veil in nearsighted confusion. I was moved.

"Can you believe it?" she asked.

Oh, I believed.

"What kind of jerk," she continued, "what kind of lunatic would wear eyeglasses for her wedding picture?"

"Perhaps," I said, staring at the little bride, "perhaps she just wanted to see."

"Good God," the young woman said, "for my wedding pictures—"

"You wear eyeglasses?"

"For my wedding pictures—"

"You're going to be married?" I asked. She was so young. She was my age.

"Why, yes," the young woman said. Lifting the finger that had touched the bride, she flashed a rhinestone ring before me. "It's temporary," she added.

"Uh," I said.

For a while we sat in dull discomfort, admiring her ring and scrutinizing the myopic bride. Then, as politely as I could, I excused myself and returned to my want ads. But I couldn't bear to look at them again, and feeling somehow renewed, as if there might be a little bridal house waiting somewhere for me, I flipped over to the rentals.

"Oh my God," the young woman said.

I dropped the rentals and stared across to her paper, expecting, perhaps, a bride with an eyepatch. But she hadn't turned the page. She said, "Oh my God, are you looking for a place to live?"

"Why . . . why yes," I said.

"What a coincidence!"

2

Her name was Yvette Bigelow and she was looking for a roommate. I couldn't believe my good fortune. She could, and with the rapid raising of one eyebrow and a sort of steady ho-hum, she began to tell me about "our" apartment. It seemed her father had set her up in a small place and she wouldn't be married for months. Her fiancé, Michael, was an actor and looking for work and, well, I knew how it was.

I did.

He had all sorts of prospects but none, at the moment, appealed to him. And while he went gallivanting around, she, Yvette—her dead mother's name—had absolutely nothing to do. Zilch. And her father, "the beast," barely gave her any spending cash. Just change. Could I believe that? Just change?

I could.

She couldn't, and what she was looking for was someone to kick in a tidbit toward the rent—oh, God, she'd figure out all the financial details later—well, it could be a divine life. How much did I have?

I cautiously mentioned my savings. A small stake. Something to set me up until I found—

"I mean," she interrupted, "in dollars and cents."

I mumbled, "A few hundred."

She scratched the air with invisible figures. "Perhaps," she said, "between your savings and my father, you wouldn't even have to get a job for a while."

"I wouldn't," I said, insanely believing her.

"Well, just take a look for yourself," she said.

She pointed to her invisible figures. I studied the air.

"Who knows," she continued, "if we're careful—"

"How long?"

Arbitrarily, she estimated, "Two, maybe three months."

"And tell me about the apartment," I said.

Slowly, as if addressing a foreigner, she designed it with words, lingering over my share. "Why don't you just take a look for yourself," she suggested. "Unless, of course, you have something else to do?"

Through the streets of New York, I followed this complete stranger home. For a while I loped beside her devil-may-care, but once we passed my gloomy boarding house and the familiar windows of the local cafeteria, I found myself longing to take her hand. It was past noon now and all the sidewalks were teeming with passersby. Strangers' elbows grazed me arbitrarily and hawkers cried viciously at our backs. In front of store windows, whole crowds got bottlenecked. Messengers whizzed by. And every now and then, from the shadows of a seedy doorway, a derelict's hand would emerge, pleading for change. Yvette wedged her way along while I trailed nervously in her wake. In formidable crowds, she'd somehow slip through. I scrutinized her every movement. There was something so spectacular about the way she walked. She barely lifted her feet. With each step her spiked heels sort of catapulted her to the next one. She turned down a quiet residential street and slouched against a building. I slouched too but it was more like a slump.

"Well," she said, "this is it."

The street was tree-lined, with flapping awnings, and posted here and there before prestigious buildings stood prestigious doormen. I was impressed.

"Over there," she said, pointing.

Completely unadorned and squeezed incongruously into the block sat a little brick box with a cracked stoop.

"It's small," she admitted, "but quaint. Definitely a find nowadays. And besides, you can't read a book by its cover."

She dragged me across the street and opened its chipped door. The entry was narrow, the staircase crooked and the ceiling peculiarly low. I followed her up several flights of steps. On a dark landing, she groped for a light switch and unlocked her door. Then she pushed me inside.

"What do you think?" she asked.

I looked around this closet of an apartment and looked at Yvette and then back at the apartment but I didn't really see it. I already had a dream fixed in my head that stood between me and reality. I asked, noticing only one bed, "Where would I sleep?"

"On the cot," Yvette said. She lifted an armful of laundry and pointed to a naked mattress below.

I studied the cot, but even with its depths and lumps,

I saw only two months of not working in its mountainous terrain.

"Try it," Yvette said.

So I walked over to it, tested it with my knee, then lay down on top of it, sinking in. The sides rose up, engulfing me. And when I climbed off again, I saw only my impression stamped into the center as if I belonged. I started to say, "I'll take it—"

But she'd collapsed on her bed and immediately began making a phone call. I discreetly sat down on the cot.

"Hello, Dad," she said, "it's me . . . your daughter, remember? Yvette."

She groaned silently, turned to me and rolled her eyes in mock disgust.

"You'll never guess what? Don't try then. I've found a roommate."

She held the receiver at arm's length and let it quack for a while.

"No, I didn't find her on the streets, Dad. We've known each other since childhood."

Immediately, I tried to envision us as childhood play-mates. From an old photograph in my mother's scrap-book, I stole me; pigtails awry, forever surrounded by a turning Hula Hoop. For Yvette, I peeled away the makeup on her animated features—she was now making diaboli-cal faces into the phone—and tried to place her on the aluminum steps of our trailer in Bakersfield. For a moment I had us both; her slouching on the searing steps and me a blur of hoops and pleats. Then she hung up with a thud.

"Dad approves."

I stood up.

"Sit down," she said. Reclining next to me, one leg draped over the edge of the cot, she raised a slender white arm and, pointing, toured me around the room by her finger tip. It grazed the arm of a record player, a lamp, an old-fashioned vanity mirror and several worn chairs facing a television set pedestaled on a bureau. Fallen clothes were scattered everywhere, and dripping over the bathroom doorknob a pair of wet silk stockings drained into a puddle. One closet had a shoe rack like a tree, its metal branches blossoming with heels and straps and patent-leather toes. In another closet, a makeshift kitchen sink teemed with china dishes, glasses and cutlery.

"We can clean this all up together," she said, embracing me, "just like sisters."

Then she sprang to her feet, rummaged through a dozen drawers, emptied several spare purses, groaned innumerable times until, hidden under the cushions of a worn chair, she discovered a spare key.

"Go get your things," she said.

3

If money could have been kissed, if my coins weren't soiled and a hundred hands hadn't touched every dollar, I might have necked with my savings. I was delighted by my prospects. I raced through the streets, actually handed a derelict a dime, and bounded up the steps to my old room. Immediately I laid out all my money. It looked impressive. I admired it for a moment, congratulating myself on my thrift and all the things I'd denied myself, a soda now and then, etc., etc. Then, for the umpteenth time, I began to count it. I carefully tallied up the bills, put the change in my pockets and hid the traveler's checks in a secret compartment in my luggage. I chucked all my clothes on top and, using my weight, fastened the latches. Then, nostalgically, I glanced one last time around the room, placed the key on the bureau, panicked that I'd left the wrong one, opened the door and quietly walked out. A gloomy boarder was loitering in the hallway.

"You don't remember me," I said obnoxiously, "but I was your neighbor." Humiliated by her astonished look, I placed my hand on her shoulder, adding, "I'm sure things will work out for you too."

Then I fled.

At the apartment, I opened the door with my spare key.

"I'm home," I announced.

But Yvette was nowhere in sight. So, somewhat disappointed, I put my suitcase in the closet, my toothbrush in a holder, made up the cot, got undressed and climbed into a pair of striped pajamas. I said to myself, "This is my second week in New York and I think . . . I think I'm already different." Then I got up to examine my new home. I borrowed a pair of Yvette's slippers and scuffed over to her vanity mirror. Family photographs were taped to the glass; an infant Yvette, a pouting toddler Yvette, Yvette embraced in the arms of her father, a first bicycle, a first kiss, two Yvettes superimposed and a strip of wallet-sized Yvettes giggling into the lens.

I opened a drawer. I was fascinated by this woman and somewhere, beneath a panty or two, beyond an open cylinder of mascara, under a rotting apple core, I was hoping to find some object the better to grasp her by.

Nothing.

I suddenly couldn't stop myself. I opened another. I shut the first. I rifled through a bag of various beauty supplies. I picked the pockets of a crumpled-up blouse. The ceiling creaked and for a moment, my heart almost stopped beating. I lay down. I think I proclaimed my own innocence aloud. My heart was still fluttering so I closed my lids and forced myself to think pleasant thoughts; my savings materialized, quadrupling before my eyes; then a dollar, like a leaf, floated out of nowhere and landed on a wallet that had absolutely no identification. I pulled the sheets up to my chin and slowly, very slowly, dropped off to sleep.

From beneath the sheets I awoke to the sound of whispers. I opened my eyes and stared across the room. It was now dark but on the bed, curled under the arcing light of a street lamp, I could see the gently tossing figure of Yvette. She was wrapped in piles and piles of blankets. The blankets were twisted and rolled around her like a gigantic hand holding her down. Finger-like mounds bent over her shape. But from one of those mounds, I saw three arms protruding. Then a pair of passing headlights revealed the soles of four feet. Discreetly, I rolled over. I feigned sleep. I closed one eye and put the sheets back over my head. I even tossed an arm out at a peculiar angle and curled my legs up. Through a gap in the sheets, I studied the wall beside me. I studied it so intently that I almost dozed off. But every now and then, as if tormented by dreams, I'd fling myself in their direction.

Hours passed. I must have flipped, rolled, dozed a dozen times, because when I looked up again it was morning and the room was absolutely still. The venetian blinds were tilted down and light fell like bars over the furniture. Yvette was still asleep, alone now, with the blanket half over her. The sun only reached her exposed feet.

I sat up. I wanted to rush across the room and examine evidence of the night before; an extra dent in the pillows would have satisfied me. Slowly, discreetly, I got to my feet and began tiptoeing toward her bed. I hardly breathed as I stood over her childlike body. A row of red nails creased a tiny breast. Her lips were parted in sleeper's awe. I examined the pillows. Indentations were everywhere. A stream of her orange hair contoured some. I wasn't quite sure what I was looking for so discreetly. I lifted the covers.

She gaped, stretched, sat up, lay down and immediately fell back asleep. By then I was up against the bathroom door, groping for the handle. It turned without my touching it and, through a gust of steam, a naked man's leg emerged like an apparition, followed by a dripping face.

"Hello," he said.

"Who are you?"

"Who am I?"

He stepped out of the bathroom, leaning his nude body unabashedly against the doorjamb. In the startling light, every muscle glistened. I didn't know what to do with my eyes. Large rivulets of water were dribbling down his chest, magnifying hairs as they went. For one insane moment, I hypnotically watched them.

"Didn't Yvette explain?"

"Explain what?" I asked. Then it occurred to me, so I quickly averted my eyes and extended a hand. "You must be Yvette's fiancé. How do you do?"

"I'm what?" he said. "Yvette!"

A groan emanated from the sheets and Yvette groggily sat up.

Money

"Is this a joke?" he asked, pointing at me. "I want her out today!"

Yvette suggested we change places, so on tiptoe I slithered past his naked torso and politely shut the door behind me. I flushed the toilet several times to offer them privacy. Then, putting my ear to the keyhole, I listened.

"Besides," Yvette was saying, "you'll hardly even notice her."

4

He definitely noticed me. From behind a set of fastidious nails which he preened continuously, his arrogant eyes watched my every move. Propped against Yvette's pillows, he was now clad in a skimpy lap robe, his muscular flanks exposed. I had my pajamas buttoned to my throat and was trying to dissolve in a corner. Yvette flitted between us.

"Lena," she said, "meet Mike."

He tossed me a forbidding look.

"Shake hands," she insisted.

Under her scrutiny, I glumly approached the bed and submerged my hand into his. The moons of his nails were dazzling.

"How do you do," I said.

"How do you do," he said.

"Well," Yvette sighed, "now that that's resolved!" And pirouetting around us, she draped herself in a sheet and offered to cook us both breakfast.

"That's awfully kind," I said.

"It's a miracle," Mike said.

Over the makeshift kitchen, a cupboard door banged open. In the brilliant light, toasters and toaster ovens, percolators and waffle irons gleamed silver. I'd never seen so many appliances.

"Gifts," Yvette explained.

"From her father," Mike said.

I sat down at the table between them, unable to take my eyes off the appliances. They were lined up in pairs like Noah's animals and when she pulled down the percolator, its mate, a smaller Mr. Coffee, appeared behind it.

"Don't you think it's peculiar?" he asked.

I thought it was wonderful. With a syringe-like machine, Yvette scrambled eggs inside their shells. A bubble of coffee rose in the percolator, under a glowing coil slices of bread changed into toast.

"As a matter of fact," he continued, "everything in here is a present from Dad. Except you and me, of course."

"And Lena's belongings," Yvette added.

"Which Yvette will get to very, very soon."

"We're going to help you unpack," she announced.

"That's awfully kind," I said.

A plate of half-cooked eggs was placed before me. "Eat up," she said. She smiled.

I tried, attempting to capture the loose eggs with my fork.

"Delicious?" Mike asked. He sat down beside me. "Personally," he said, "I never eat breakfast."

"That's because you're never up," Yvette said.

She nibbled on the toast, he played with his spoon and I slurped up the eggs. After a bite or two, my plate was whisked away.

"Finished?" they asked.

"Well, actually I was—"

"Good," Yvette said. She prodded Mike with her elbow. "Why don't you fetch Lena's suitcase?"

From a dark corner of the closet, next to the branches of the shoe tree, he pulled out my suitcase.

"Let's see what you've got hidden in there," she said, unfastening the latches.

A heap of disorganized clothing was piled in the center. Shoes lined the edges. One lone glove had worked its way to the top and, for a moment, looked as if a body lay crumpled beneath it.

She started unpacking. She rummaged through everything, casting it to one side. Shoes were tossed in the closet, shirts indiscriminately draped over hangers. I'd bend every now and then to offer a hand but she'd simply brush it aside. So I stood back awkwardly, watching. Then suddenly I realized she was as curious about me as I was about her. I couldn't believe it. I was actually flattered. And for a brief moment, I waited in expectation for her to stumble upon some mysterious object we could both better grasp me by.

We found nothing. The suitcase was practically empty. She left the dregs untouched and began fingering all the linings. A used toothpick. A broken bobby pin. The crumpled address of some distant cousin. I almost apologized. Then, under the secret compartment, she discovered my savings.

"Look at this!" she said, holding up the thin folder of traveler's checks. "Did you see these, Mike? Look how farsighted Lena was." Then she began fanning herself with them, adding, "And how cautious."

"I was worried about thieves," I said.

Part Two:
Fast Money

5

Yvette helped me find a safe hiding place for my savings, and during the next several days we lived in a sort of cramped domestic bliss, hardly bothering to leave the apartment at all. Mike simply ignored me, as I did him, and under Yvette's steady gaze, we managed to coexist with only the slightest friction. Our sleeping arrangements were somewhat awkward but I often feigned sleep and, after Yvette's horrified look, stopped complaining about the creaking of their springs. I did everything I could to become as inconspicuous as possible. I rearranged my cot so that my feet faced them. I rarely rolled over no matter what I heard. And when I awoke thirsty at midnight, I'd lie dehydrating on my cot. If I was voyeuristic, I wasn't after dark.

I was much more fascinated by their wakeful selves. Their lifestyle struck me as spectacular. They hardly did anything. They rarely left their bed, and when they did, they floated around the apartment in somnambulistic postures. Meals were devoured, regardless of correct feeding times. The television set blared from morning till night. If an errand had to be run, they'd complain about it for hours.

"I'll do it!" I'd volunteer, hoping to become a part of them.

And off I'd trot to the corner grocery store with a list that was thoroughly humiliating—cakes, popcorn, soda pops, et cetera. I'd throw in a lettuce just to be able to face the grocer. Nobody ever offered to reimburse me.

Yvette was extraordinarily kind, though, profusely thanking me for the errands and constantly praising my good points to Mike. I was pliable, helpful and quiet, besides being almost visionary in collecting such a savings. I lapped all this up. Sometimes she'd invite me into the big bed next to her (Mike glaring at me from behind a pillow) and we'd stare at the ceiling or she'd stretch across my legs to flip the TV channels while I, in a fit of unbecoming giggles, belittled all the programs. Her laughter was flawless. I could have lain supine under the arc of her body indefinitely. By late afternoon, we'd all be in a tangle of sheets watching the walls of our apartment turn savagely bright. The screen had already paled with the last spokes of daylight, returning to its original underwater green, and outside the city became only fleeting sounds that filtered up through our open blinds. Sometimes I'd move to the window ledge to watch hats stroll by, but for the most part, I was perfectly content to absorb New York through the photographs in my tour book. Often, if Mike wasn't looking, I'd peek over the pages to absorb Yvette—standing, stooping, yawning or stretching; her movements transfixed me. One evening she helped me draft a letter home about some fictitious job, but the next day I couldn't quite bring myself to post it. And, although sorely tempted from time to time, I never counted my money in front of her.

Instead I acquired a new habit. Every morning I'd leaf through the columns of the want ads like an old woman who reads the obituaries knowing that her name can't possibly be among them. One morning, just as I had gleefully finished Secretarial Help, Yvette climbed out of bed and lay down beside me.

"Lena," she said, "I hope you're finding it comfortable here. I mean, with Mike and me."

She'd never inquired before. I said, "Absolutely."

"You seem to be having a good time."

"Are you kidding me?"

"So am I," she said.

I was very flattered.

"But," she quickly added, "how long do you think we can go on like this?"

It had never occurred to me. I simply shrugged.

"You know," she continued, "everything depends on money."

I agreed.

"And how do you think money works?"

"You earn it," I said miserably.

"Don't be naive."

She shouted for Mike who emerged half-dazed from the sheets. He spent an inordinate amount of time sleeping. We watched him sit up. Then she turned to me and placed a hand on the small of my back.

"Lena," she said, "I think it's about time we told you

how money works." She gently removed the want ads. "It works like rabbits."

"That's right," Mike agreed.

"Like rabbits," Yvette continued, "you've got to pair money. You've got to pair dollar for dollar, Lena, and let it work for you. Why, only a lunatic would try to earn it."

She stood up and sauntered over to the windows.

"Out there," she said, pulling on the string that opened the venetian blinds, "out there, the city is filled with lunatics." She urged me to look.

Across the street, two young children joyously floated bubble gum wrappers in the gutter. One had made a sail out of tin foil. A pipe cleaner sailor, with hands and feet modeled from their chewed gum, teetered from starboard. The children navigated him with their gentle breath.

"They look happy enough," Yvette said, "but it's a delusion. That one," and she pointed to the boy, "he'll probably be an accountant. And the other," she said, revolving her finger to the little girl, "she'll probably rot in some miserable office."

"In other words," Mike said, "it's hard to make money."

"But," Yvette said, "it's easy to make money make money."

They both took an elbow and guided me back to my cot. We sat in a row of three, me squeezed into the middle. Yvette placed her hand on my knee while Mike encircled my shoulders with a powerful arm. Then, slowly, sometimes talking at once, they unfolded a scheme

whereby I'd sell my traveler's checks to a forger for half
their cost, then claim that they'd been stolen and receive
a fresh new batch. These I'd immediately cash in and
we'd have one and a half times my savings.

"It's a wonderful plan," they agreed with each other.

I asked them to repeat it.

They did.

I said, "Hey, guys, you don't understand. It's all I have.
It's my life savings."

"That's just the point," Yvette said, "it *is* all you have."

"What's wrong with that?" I asked.

"What's wrong?" Yvette said.

"I'll have two, maybe three months of—"

"And then?" Yvette said.

"And then," Mike agreed.

"And then," Yvette continued, "you'll have to get yourself a job."

"And where in God's name could we possibly find a
forger?" I couldn't believe I was asking.

"It could be arranged. A friend of a friend of Mike's."

"And what if they wanted proof? What if they wanted
a police report on the stolen checks?"

"Chuck the theft part, we'll say they've been lost," Yvette
said. She leaned over and gently removed a sweaty lock
from my forehead. "These are only details, Lena. Minor
considerations. We can wing it as we go along."

6

Yvette and Mike and I sat on a subway bench waiting for our rendezvous with the forger. I'd never been in a subway before. Commuters, all with suspicious faces, surged by. Mike insisted he'd been told what the forger would look like and, every now and then, rose to meet the sudden onslaught of passengers funneling through the train doors. I rose too, but to scan these crowds for suspicious behavior: a blind man was giving directions to three young girls, a stack of yesterday's newspapers ran past on two spindly legs and someone hovered behind us reading a subway map of Philadelphia. Yvette glanced at her watch.

"My God this woman is late."

Mike sat down in a series of tics. I remained standing, pretending to become disgusted too. I trod back and forth. But actually I was numb. I was so numb that I even acquired a slight limp. Then I suddenly bent over and removed a piece of lint from Yvette's stocking.

"Sit," Yvette commanded.

I sat. All the suspicious faces instantly arranged themselves behind me. I kept twisting.

Mike said, "We've been stood up."

They both stood up. I remained on the bench, my fingers gripping the slats. Then, over the unnerving din of the station, I heard a voice ask, "Lena?"

And from under the subway map of Philadelphia, a hand was extended. It was the forger's hand.

The streets of Philadelphia were unfolded into a barricade. Yvette and Mike and I were squeezed behind its boulevards. The map's key was decorated by Liberty Bells over which the startling face of the forger protruded. Her features looked temporary: over the stubble of where her brows had been, penciled brows were drawn. Glued eyelashes hung from her lids, and along the cavities of her cheeks were painted flushed circles of health. Her lips were shaped at random, a wig sat askew under her hat. With trembling fingers, I handed her my traveler's checks.

"How much?" she asked.

Suddenly, I couldn't remember. A phantom total kept dissolving before my eyes. The hours and hours I'd spent totaling and totaling these checks only crystallized into the image of me, temporarily bent over my money.

Yvette said, "Four hundred and fifty." Exactly what Mike told them.

"Is that correct?" she asked, turning to me.

"Anything she says," I said.

The forger began to tally up my checks. From behind an ear, she pulled out the stub of a pencil and, after salivating for a while on its point, scrawled the amount, slicing it in half and writing my figure in cash above it.

"Agreed?" she asked.

I agreed. Mike held his hands out for the cash but the forger brushed them aside, saying, "Not you and not here."

Then she turned her head around, as if looking for something, and the dominant blur of her startling features left only a mask in the air.

"Come with me."

Alone, I was lured into a vacant corridor. At any minute I anticipated a dozen thugs slinking over the barrier of the tracks or popping out from behind a cigarette machine. But we stood unmolested in the shadows while the forger produced a scrap of paper from a purse slung over her shoulder.

"Sign it," she commanded.

I did, carefully taking the pencil from her hands. My letters arced and spilled over one another and out of their ends, a shriveled bumpy line protruded. I turned the paper around for her to see it but she completed the circle until my signature faced me again. Then, in identical proportion but upside down, I watched her duplicate it. With the opposite hand, she even spilled my letters and matched that ending line. I stared at the paper. I scrutinized the differences. I ran my eyes across my names, leaping and blinking over the gaps. But it was as if I'd written them both.

"Again," the forger commanded.

My pencil immediately took flight. I had to mouth my name in order to remember it. I waited in awe for her to perform again but this time she simply held our signature up against the one on my traveler's checks. With professional scrutiny, a penciled brow rose slightly.

"Well?" I asked bravely, "how did we do?"

"We did," the forger smiled, "just fine."

"I'm so glad," I said.

"Your money now," the forger said. She pulled out my payment, a wad of bills rolled in a rubber band. "Wait one whole week," she said, dangling it before me. "Then you can report the loss of your checks."

I nodded in agreement, cautiously taking the wad.

"Count it," she insisted.

I did, running my fingers quickly around the bills. I turned to assure her that it was all there but the forger had disintegrated into the crowds. For a moment I thought I caught a glimpse of her elbows parting a row of school children. But then a train rumbled by and in the hollow of its aftermath, I was just as sure I'd seen her features streaked across one of its windows.

Half dazed, I walked back to the bench.

"Did you get it all?" Mike greeted me.

He had his arm around Yvette, his scrupulous nails drumming on her shoulder. I didn't say anything. I squeezed down between them and let him palpitate for a while. When Yvette asked kindly, "Are you all right?"

I showed her the wad of bills, still wound around each other with a rubber band.

"Well, this certainly was exhausting," she said. "Let's take a cab home."

"From the subway, Yvette?"

"Why not?" Mike said. "We've got the money."

"And besides," Yvette added, "the whole underground is riddled with thieves."

The cabbie sat behind bullet-proof glass. A blurry New York whizzed by through its bottle-thick texture. I was bolt upright, studying the meter. Yvette and Mike lounged beside me.

"Relax," Yvette commanded, "you're beginning to make me nervous, Lena."

I slumped back and crossed my still-wobbly legs. Then I fidgeted against the sticky upholstery.

"I'd never been in the subways before," I confided, as nonchalantly as I could.

"You're joking?" Yvette said.

"To be perfectly frank, this is my first time in a cab."

She was flabbergasted. "How did you ever get around?" she asked. Then she pounded on the divider. "Take this young woman through the park!"

So we squealed around the corner and began barreling through the park. Through the bullet-proof glass, everything appeared pastoral. A bric-a-brac of country shadows streamed over our laps. In the distance, I could make out flocks of elderly people feeding pigeons, and gangs of mothers tending their children. Once a ball bounced into our path but threaded safely between the tires. Here and there a sweaty child stood attached to a kite. Then, over the tree tops, the city loomed up again and, by the time we burst onto its boulevards, I was thoroughly enjoying the taxi ride. Yvette began to point out famous hotspots and restaurants.

"I recognize some of them from my tour book," I said.

7

A summer storm came and went. The sky stayed gray. That week I began to unravel. I'd lie awake each night convinced that at any moment a knock would be heard at our door—an official tap that would splinter the air. When I'd drift into sleep, claps of thunder awoke me and flashes of lightning caught me in every conceivable posture. I'd sit up and, if Yvette and Mike were asleep, I'd start pacing restlessly. One night I begged them to keep me company.

At Mike's suggestion, I took up smoking. He thought I might exhaust myself by inhaling. I didn't. After each cigarette, nauseous and dizzy, I'd flop back onto my cot to test my hopeless incapacity for sleep.

Dawns would often catch me at the window, bleary-eyed but almost serene. Outside, puddles lined the avenue. The bottoms of oily pigeons rippled across them. And every now and then, from the depths of a cloud, a momentary sun would emerge and reflect on our neighbor's window.

Then, without hope of sleep, I'd force myself under the sheets—and often doze off.

"Get up, Lena!"

Yvette was standing above me. I could barely open my eyes from my week of sleepless nights. I found it difficult to move.

"Come on, kid. Today's the day. Mike's gone to get a cab. He'll be back any minute!"

She went to the window. I coaxed myself to my feet. She opened the blinds. The street was dazzling.

I took off my pajamas, then I sat down again. I was totally drained and immediately fell into a stupor.

Yvette stood in front of her vanity holding shirt, skirt, stockings and shoes in front of her comely form. Hangers protruded like shoulders and hips from their sleeves and waistbands.

"What should I wear today?" I asked passively.

"I don't know," Yvette said. "Pick something at random, something that looks inconspicuous."

She tossed me a black and white striped shift.

"I couldn't wear that," I said. "It looks like a prisoner's outfit."

The door burst open and my hands automatically flew up to shield my nudity.

"You're not even dressed," Mike greeted me.

"We were trying to figure out what I should wear."

"You're up every night, Lena. You couldn't have figured it out then?"

"Just zip her up," Yvette said.

So, coyly, clinging to the little striped dress, I shifted from foot to foot while Mike clumsily zipped me inside. Then I actually pirouetted around, hoping, perhaps, for

a second opinion. I smoothed a wrinkle or two over my
lanky hips.

"What are you standing there for?" Mike asked.

"Doesn't she look nice," Yvette said.

"Do you really think so?"

"Go get your receipts."

From under my pillow, I pulled out the papers for my—
stolen? lost? sold?—traveler's checks and, pocketing them
securely, descended to the streets below.

8

We must have cased a dozen banks. The city was never so enormous, and banks never so abundant. They were like bookends on every block. Yvette and Mike bickered over which one to choose.

"Well?" Yvette said, "what do you think?"

We were outside a neighborhood branch. I studied it in the rearview mirror, reluctantly agreed, and we scrambled out of the cab, following a young couple with a chubby little boy inside.

"Hey, guys," I said, looking around, "I don't know if I can go through with this. Perhaps you could do it for me?"

"I don't think so," Yvette said.

"Just get in line," Mike said.

I didn't budge. Immediately I offered another plan. "Perhaps you could come with me?"

"No," Yvette said. Then she pointed to the chubby little boy who was now holding a ceramic pig and bravely entering the maze of brass posts and velvet ropes alone.

So I lined up behind the little boy.

"May I help you?" a teller asked.

"Yes," the boy said, "I want to open an account."

"That's wonderful," the teller said, "that's so responsible. Your parents must be very proud."

"I guess," the boy said.

His parents ogled him from behind the velvet ropes.

"May I have your pig?"

"I guess," the boy said.

The teller took his pig. She turned it on its back and tried to pry off the plastic stopper.

"I can't seem to get this off," she said, scraping and scratching at the belly with her nails. "What shall we do now?"

"I don't know," the boy said.

"I have an idea." The teller left and returned with a hammer.

The little boy blanched. "Couldn't we just put him in a safe?"

"I'm sorry," the teller said, "but we only take cash or checks here. Would you like to do it?"

"No."

"Should I?"

"No."

"Your parents?"

"No."

I thought I was losing my mind. "I'll do it!" I volunteered. I took the hammer and smashed the pig to smithereens.

They both looked at me in silence.

I turned to the boy. He was now staring at the remains of his pig. For a moment, his little fingers worked frantically, trying to put it back together.

"That was awfully helpful of you," the teller said as soon as the boy had gone. "What can we do for you?"

I showed her my receipts and told her I'd lost my traveler's checks.

"That's no problem," she assured me, "but I'll have to get the manager."

She signaled a handsome young man and I followed him around the lines of people, past Yvette and Mike and a security guard into a plush office. A box of doughnuts sat on the desk.

"Help yourself," he said. "This will only take a moment."

Alone in the office, I devoured the doughnuts. I couldn't stop myself. I ate a chocolate one, then one with jimmies on top, then two sprinkled with powdered sugar.

"Well, everything seems to be in order." The young man had returned with a questionnaire.

"I'm so relieved," I said.

"But," he continued, taking a seat beside me, "I'll have to know where it was you lost the checks."

Suddenly I was feeling nauseous.

"Think carefully," he said.

Through waves of nausea, I tried to conjure up an image of New York. I ransacked my memories of the photographs in my tour book, hoping to select a likely place, but the shots of towering skyscrapers, glittering façades seemed completely inappropriate.

"Can you remember where you've been lately?"

I thought of where I'd been lately.

"You look a little peaked."

"It's the doughnuts."

"Oh well," he said, scrutinizing the empty box, "why don't we leave that question blank for the moment?"

He handed me his card.

"As soon as you're feeling better, I'll be expecting your call."

"Of course," I lied.

Then, rising to his feet, he ushered me out the door.

On the ledge of the teller's window, a fresh new batch of traveler's checks sat waiting. All I had to do was scrawl my signatures again.

9

That was terrific," Yvette said. "Breaking the kid's bank was a stroke of genius."

Mike patted me on the shoulder. They insisted we celebrate. A fancy meal, perhaps?

I mentioned my nausea.

A film? A party for three?

"Well, actually," I said, "there is something I'd really like to do."

"Yes?"

"I'd like to have my picture taken on the Empire State Building."

"Are you kidding?" Mike said.

"Is it still standing?" Yvette asked.

From inside my purse I pulled out my tour book, opening to the first page, a 1948 black-and-white collage of all New York's landmarks. Statues were glued together, sunrises burst from all sides, a bridge spanned the borders, and out of its trestles the Empire State Building loomed in silhouette. I read them the italicized blurb, *photographs 50 cents.*

"Well I'll be damned," Yvette said.

"Prices have gone up," I admitted, "but"—and I chucked

my new traveler's checks on top of the collage—"money is no object now."

Against the backdrop of Manhattan, surrounded by aggressive girl scouts elbowing for a view, I posed without my glasses and paid a little stooped photographer five dollars for the Polaroid snapshot. Then, next to a farmer's family who had also had their pictures taken, I waited impatiently for mine to develop. Yvette and Mike waited impatiently too. The first thing we saw inside the white deckle edges was me like a speck. I couldn't make out my features yet. Then, creeping along the horizon, a line like a child's drawing of a metropolis materialized, darkened, and the tip of the island was formed. We could see the wharves. Next rooftops wavered into focus and a speck of dirt became a pigeon. I was still a little apparition-like, but my features were growing more distinct. I recognized some annoying freckles and a curl that never fell into place. Then the hairs of my cocked eyebrow stood out and slowly, very slowly, a smile formed on my photogenic lips.

"Well, guys," I said, "what do you think?"

They looked at the photograph, looked at me, and back at the photograph.

"It looks just like you, Lena."

"I think so too," said the farmer's wife.

It did. Those annoying freckles had now multiplied into a constellation scattered over the bridge of my nose. Yvette's black and white striped dress surrounded me like a cage. My legs were held together but only my bony knees touched. And one hand thrown out in a gesture of sophistication now appeared like a scrawny arm groping through the dress's bars.

"I don't like it," I said.

"What's wrong with it?" Yvette said.

I tried to explain, pointing to my freckles, her dress, the legs. Then I showed her the scrawny arm, saying, "I think it looks like a claw, Yvette. I'd like another picture taken."

"That's ridiculous," said the farmer's wife.

"It's a waste of money," Mike added.

"Let me see! Let me see!" her children screamed.

So I stood there while each one of her children studied the snapshot. They all thought I looked fine.

That evening Yvette insisted we scotch-tape the photograph to the wall above my cot. It was my first decoration in our apartment. I sat staring moodily at its placement, my pose, the idiot grin on my lips. Then, subtly, she suggested I go to bed. I wanted to discuss the photograph some more, perhaps extract another compliment or two. But Mike had been pacing back and forth, anxiously waiting for my eyelids to droop. I tossed him a resentful look, feigned a yawn, climbed under my sheets, glanced at my new traveler's checks, the photograph, shut my lids and was banished to sleep.

Part Three:
Loose Money

10

Left and right, right and left we dashed through my money. Bills were peeled off my wad, change tumbled from my pockets. I was the center of attraction. I acquired the tone of an accountant, the vocabulary of a banker. I tallied, approximated, multiplied, divided and subtracted—and subtracted and subtracted. Yvette told me I had a real aptitude for numbers. And I held each of her compliments in reverence.

On a schoolgirl tablet, I kept a list of our expenditures. If I questioned any, Yvette simply complimented me on my handwriting. If I hemmed at some trivial purchase, Mike had a zillion reasons for its necessity. And if I hawed before the cashing of another traveler's check, there was always an excuse at hand: change for tokens, change for automats, change for the cigarettes I now devoured.

Yvette and Mike and I became a trio of shifting relationships. We were Yvette and Mike with Yvette's roommate tagging along; Yvette and me with Yvette's boyfriend tagging along; me and Mike bickering over who got to stand, sit, walk next to Yvette; me alone trying to curb their spending sprees; one or the other leaping into a cab, a restaurant, a photo booth; two heads kissing in front of the lenses (I was in gloomy profile); six hands trying to count my change at once. In those days of disorganized spending, I hadn't yet perceived the physical complications of being a trio. I simply relied on luck and the magnetic quality of my coin-filled pockets to lure Yvette to my side.

She was the ideal consumer—awestruck over bins of bargains, entranced by alluring ads—and I was consumed with vying for more and more of her attention. Whenever Mike embraced her—and he was forever embracing her—I'd quickly chirp up with the promise of some extravagant sale in some extravagant shop if only she'd be quick about it.

Boutiques, beauty parlors, negligee shops all became havens for me. Inside their perfumed atmospheres, amid the rows of silken hosiery, I'd finally get to be alone with Yvette. For hours I'd insist she thumb through the racks, all the time stealing triumphant glances at Mike pacing outside in the hot sun.

I became innocently manipulative. During monster matinees which Mike insisted he had to attend to study some actor drooling through bandages or fur, I'd immediately feign such fright that Yvette permitted me to sit in the middle. There, under romantic werewolf moons, in flashes of demonic lightning, I'd study her—profile aglow, shoulders luminous. Mike's hand would often creep around me to paw her, but it was always my hand she clasped when those sad drooling creatures appeared.

I began relying more and more on her vanity. After hours in those pitch-black theaters, we'd emerge into startling afternoons so sun-drenched and disorienting that our reflections in a shop window would appear strange to us.

"Good God, Yvette," I'd advise, "I think you should have your hair done."

And we'd abandon Mike on street corners, at subway stops, his gloomy figure descending into the darkness, and run off to mysterious pink parlors where the vast array of machinery seemed infinitely more terrifying than any celluloid monster. I'd help her pick out a hairdo—beehive, flip, bangs, what-have-you—then wait for her to be transformed. Staring at Yvette under the conical shape of the dryers, her fingers splayed while some pale woman clipped and painted her nails, I had never felt so happy. And when the nets and curlers were removed and a stiff curl cascaded down her flushed cheeks, I'd sign away another traveler's check with a penmanship that Yvette never failed to compliment me on:

"I think your signature is getting more mature, Lena."

Leafing through my tattered schoolgirl tablet dated 1965, I can still make out the faded list of our purchases and recall moments of innocent bliss that can only be conveyed by that childish handwriting. Halfway down the first page a flower, daisy I think, dots the *i* of *sanitary napkins* and a grinning face fills the *o* of *comic books*. Penciled hearts surround everything Yvette bought. And she bought a lot—a backless dress for an occasion we'd never attend, spiked heels upon which only an acrobat could balance, colorful scarves, bras, slips, garter belts (we both abhorred girdles), and seven tiny panties with the name of every day embroidered on them.

I became more familiar with the cartography of department stores than I ever did with the streets of New York. While Yvette shopped and shopped, I, from a vista of mezzanines, would take in the landscape of hatracks and wig hills, mangled bargains in traffic jams of grabbing arms, a shoe display where summer sandals dangled from metal stands like children from jungle gyms. Sometimes we'd be the last to leave. A kindly floorwalker would have to escort us through the revolving doors. Then, hours overdue, Yvette still flushed from the delirium of buying and me sweating under all the packages, having dilly-dallied past more shop windows, we'd finally burst through our own door to Mike's furious stare.

During those days, I was so intent on making Yvette happy that I failed to notice that he was accompanying us less and less. Every morning we'd have to tiptoe quietly out past his steady snoring, and when we'd return, the only change in the apartment was his position of sleep. He didn't even take an interest in what we bought. When Yvette modeled her every-day-of-the-week underwear in front of us (I preferred Magenta Sunday), he'd merely groan, "So what?"

After slipping her into that backless dress, balancing her on those stiletto heels, I'd flop back gawking, but Mike would only sneer. From his throne of pillows he belittled her flips, criticized her beehives, passed judgment on her bangs. And once, when she surprised him with a turtleneck dickey, claiming that all the young actors were wearing them, he didn't even bother to try it on.

"I'm bored," he announced one morning. "With you, Yvette. With your clothes. And especially with her. I'm so bored, I'm Chairman of the Bored."

From that moment on, he simply refused to leave the bed. When Yvette tried to climb out of it, he grabbed her by her delicate wrist, threatening that if she went out shopping again, he'd leave her.

Yvette burst into dry sobs. I had to escort her into the bathroom. There she wept openly, collapsing on my shoulder.

"Just let him rot," I said.

But she shook her head no.

"Why doesn't he occupy himself by looking for a job?"

"He's an actor," Yvette sobbed.

"An actor?"

I brushed aside a couple of wisps of her orange hair, peering through the crack in the doorway. I could only make out Mike's immobile hand dangling over the edge of the bed, like a corpse's.

I said, "An actor? Yvette, the only way he's ever going to get on stage is as a prop."

But she ignored me. She was examining her swollen eyes in the mirror. The rims were aflame, the lashes bunched together like star points. Coal-black mascara ran down her cheeks.

"I look awful."

"No you don't," I lied.

Money

She used my pajama sleeve to mop up her cheeks. Then, turning on the cold water faucet, she bravely submerged her face and neck. I lifted up the bulk of her hair, astonished by the delicacy of her nape. A vertebra the size of a quail egg glistened with water. I offered her my other sleeve.

"Thank you."

"It's nothing."

She shrugged slightly, pecked me on the cheek, and returned to Mike's bed.

I knew it was hopeless. Collapsing on my cot, surrounded by my piles of coins, my neatly stacked bills, I watched her snuggle up against him—and drift away from me.

11

During the next several days, I spent hours on my cot hoping for a sign of life from Yvette: an open eye to stare back at, her old bubbly self skimming through the advertisements for bargains. But Mike had her pinned under his comatose arms. I didn't dare mention a department store or sale. Around noon he'd emerge from their sheets, motioning me to keep quiet, then examine the clock in horror and tumble back into the bed beside her. In my lonely state I'd have done anything to please her. Oh, I was quiet and I was good and sometimes I'd force my nerve-wrought body into the curvature of sleep. I think I hoped that in some brief interval between dreams she might awaken and see that I, too, could fit in. And then, I gradually did. Out of weariness, I began my own dormant marathon.

This was a typical day: a forgotten dream or two, a groggy face lifted in a daze, meals that were so brief we devoured them from cans or had pimply-faced adolescents deliver pizzas to our door, an afternoon nap and, for the climax of my day, feigning exhaustion in the early evening because Mike insisted they have a little more privacy.

Money

One morning I awoke with a slight headache. At first
I dismissed it as the result of restless sleep. But the next
day it had doubled in intensity. Yvette gave me an ice
pack to put over my eyes. Day after day it grew worse.
I woke in pools of melted ice. My neck became stiff. My
nerves grew short. My skull ached from temples to base.
Trifling noises completely unnerved me. If Mike merely
snored, I'd start snapping viciously at him. If Yvette tried
to take his side, I'd begin ranting. For hours I'd lie in a
ball on my cot, clutching my head and watching their
healthy bodies with annoyance.

"Good God, can't you two think of anything to do but
sleep!"

Or, if their bed springs creaked:

"Well, well, if I only felt better, I'd certainly do something more productive with my time!"

Sleep had become impossible. I'd pace the early morning hours away. Finally I couldn't stand it any more. Yvette
and Mike lay on their backs with their eyes glazed over.
I followed their lines of vision but couldn't fathom what
they were looking at. Yvette's stare ended at a bed post,
Mike's at a wall. All the various appliances had been turned
on. Coffee percolated, a piece of charred bread sat smoking in the toaster, the television set blared and a record
was suspended over the turntable. Suddenly I couldn't
bear to see Yvette like this any longer. Suddenly I couldn't
stand my own life. I sat down next to her.

"Let's do something today. Let's spend some more
money."

"No." Yvette shook her head. Then she turned her dazed

145

expression toward Mike. "I'd like to be alone with him for a while."

"You what?" I said.

"Mike and I need a little time together."

For a moment I was on the brink of ranting about how they did nothing else, but there was something so tragic about her eyes—red, dazed, blank, a small swelling of tears behind her lids—that I grabbed my bottle of aspirin and fled to the streets.

The city had already begun to heat up. I wandered up and down the boulevards without purpose. If I spied a shop that Yvette and I had been in, I turned a corner. I avoided all department stores. Whenever I passed a pair of people or a group of friends, I felt utterly alone. I convinced myself that everyone was watching me. Now a lonely girl is walking down the street, now a lonely girl is sitting at a bus stop, now the pathetic thing is swallowing aspirins. By noon the heat had become so oppressive that the passersby looked as forlorn as I did. One fat man was trying to squeeze himself into a square of shade. Pedestrians trudged by miserably. I took pleasure in our common bond. Even with my throbbing headache I'd have been content to watch them all day, but a woman walked up to me, dropped open her jaw and pointed to her toothless gums.

"I have to go to the dentist," she announced.

I began riding the air-conditioned buses. The view from my seat, of sweltering heads, was pleasing. Transferring from this bus to that, I'd elbow my way to a window and sit down between people in the midst of a conversation.

Money

I didn't care. On a cross-town bus, I wormed my way between two secretaries complaining about their lives.

"I'm so confused," the first one moaned.

"So what else is new?" the other one said.

This they found incredibly funny. I thought they'd topple off their seats from laughter. I wanted to include myself.

"I seem to have missed the joke, girls."

They both looked at me in silence. I fled the bus at its next stop. A concession stand with an open grill was wavering in bands of heat. I ordered a Coke and drank it amid a flurry of sparrows bickering over a potato chip. With every other sip I devoured an aspirin. I had to rest but the thought of returning to Yvette's vacant stares was unbearable. I walked several blocks to a shady park and took a seat across from the slides, swings, rings and jungle gym. Two little girls, identical twins dressed in identical plaid jumpsuits, were hanging by their knees, dangling their little bodies. Then they plopped into the sand and grew bored.

"What should we do now?" they asked their big sister.

"I'm going to tell you a horror story," their big sister said.

"Oh, yes," the little twins cried, "tell us a horror story."

"But it's only horrible because it's true."

"Oh, we don't mind."

They climbed onto the park bench beside her. I was on the far end. I couldn't help eavesdropping.

"Once upon a time, mother didn't want either one of you," their big sister began.

147

"She didn't?" the twins cried.

"No," their big sister said, "she wished you'd disap-
pear."

"When was that?" they demanded.

"How old are you now?" their sister asked.

Each raised four chubby fingers.

"Nope," their sister said.

They lowered a finger, blotting out a year.

"Keep going," she said.

I stood up. I actually ran back to the apartment. When
I got there it looked as if Yvette hadn't moved all day.
She was all alone sitting up in bed watching a fly climb
her leg.

"Is Mike out?" I asked, stepping inside.

In one deft movement, she squashed the fly.

"No," she said, pointing.

Sprawled under *my* sheets, his unshaven cheek denting
my pillow, his arms and legs wound around *my* mattress,
Mike was asleep on *my* cot.

"Up we go, mister!" I said, with vehemence.

"Shhhh," Yvette whispered harshly. "Mike's depressed."

"Oh God," I said. I lifted up a corner of my sheet and
stared at his immobile body. "Perhaps he should move
about more."

12

That night I had to sleep with Yvette in the big bed. Mike hadn't emerged from my sheets. Yvette went to sleep early, but I stood holding a sort of vigil over my lost cot. Eventually my headache forced me to lie down, so I crept onto the narrow margin of mattress beside Yvette. At first I didn't dare breathe. With a sleeper's disregard, she'd curled herself spoon-fashion on my portion of the bed, the curve of her spine an inch or two from my side. For several minutes I was on the brink of awakening her to demand my natural sleeping space. I waited anxiously for a yawn, a snore, an excuse to nudge her from my side.

Minutes passed. The heat from her body enveloped me. My legs itched. A strand of her hair disturbed my breathing. From time to time I'd whisper, "Yvette, are you asleep?"

But she didn't budge. I wasn't sure what to do. Her contented breathing began to annoy me. I tapped several times on her shoulder but she only moaned. Desperately, I kicked away the sheets to awaken her.

And there, an inch or two from my side, lay the most beautiful sight I'd ever seen: a translucent Yvette, with bands of moonlight shimmering across thighs and hips that seemed to turn forever in that pale light, and a white breast—the purest white I'd ever seen—spilling over her ribs. For several minutes I lay perfectly still, frightened that the pounding of my heart would disturb her.

Then, stealing a glance toward Mike, I reached out and touched her. She didn't move, recoil, scream. Only a slight moan rose from her chest. Under my hand, each rib seemed miraculously formed. I watched her breasts rise and fall. Then, very gently, I buried my face in the hollow of her arm.

"Yvette," I said the next morning, "I think my head-aches are gone."

"So is Mike," Yvette said.

I was still groggy from sleep and astonished by the placement of my head. It rested on one of Yvette's breasts. Regretfully I lifted it to look. Across the apartment, un-der a mountain of sheets, my little cot lay empty. Several closet doors were open and hangers were scattered over the floor. I lay my head back down. I said, "Don't worry, Yvette. Mike will be back. We haven't spent all of my money."

"A lot you care," she said.

I didn't care. I wanted to luxuriate for a while in the softness of her breast. If I could have effaced Mike from her memory, I'd have given all my money.

She fidgeted beneath me.

"Could you please stop breathing all over me, Lena."

I stopped breathing.

"And could you please remove your head. It's beginning to annoy me."

I removed my head.

"Well," she said, "aren't you curious why he left?"

I wasn't curious at all. Under my cheeks lay the pillows on which she'd slept. They emitted a faint aroma of Yvette.

"He left," Yvette continued, "because, because, because—"

I knew that if I didn't feign curiosity, sober myself from the stupor of Yvette, I'd lose her forever. I mumbled, "Because?"

"Because"—Yvette burst out crying—"I asked him to marry me!"

I was stunned.

"Oh God, Lena, what possessed me?" she sobbed.

Slowly I inched my way back onto her breast. She clung to my head. I said philosophically, "Everyone's capable of a mistake, Yvette."

"What's that supposed to mean?"

"I just don't think he's right for you."

"But I thought," she cried, "I thought he loved me."

Bravely, from the soft depths of her breast, I confided, "I love you."

"Oh, I know," Yvette said. "I love you too, Lena. We've gotten very close as roommates. But it's just not the same."

My head sank down once again.

"Mike is everything to me!" Her head was thrashing slightly. A tiny blue vein quivered on her neck. "I just can't see any future without him!" she sobbed.

Then a miracle happened. She turned her attention to me. Lifting my face in her delicate palms, she asked, "Are you crying, Lena?"

Oh, I was crying. My vision had clouded and tears wound down my cheeks. One splashed onto her breast.

"I never realized," she said.

"Yes?"

"I never knew you were so concerned about my problems."

13

Problems. As a child I remember the thrill of spending hours unpuzzling them in an old textbook of my mother's. How many apples and oranges equal what? Did Mary receive the correct change? Who stole the cherry pie if Tom, Dick and Harry can only lie once in their confessions? But the ones that most intrigued me, the ones that brought a little lump to my throat, were those that calculated impending doom. If a train left the station at such and such a time, and a drunken brakeman fell asleep at his post, at what hour, minute, second would it collide with the passenger train that chugged blissfully through the night?

A whole day passed without a word from Mike. Yvette refused to leave her bed. I lay next to her, calculating all the variables that might delete Mike from her memory and replace him with me. Can oranges be miraculously transformed into apples? How many hours did I try? At what minute, second did I lose hope? There was a brief moment, in the dusty haze of the afternoon, when I almost grasped the complexity of my dream. But then it vanished and I stared down at Yvette, as if somewhere under her dazed expression lay a baffling but extractable answer.

That evening I did my best to make her comfortable. I piled pillows under her head and changed the sheets as a nurse might change those under an invalid. Then, tearing myself from her side, I began to cook us dinner. From the freezer I selected two frozen lamb chops and lined up all the necessary appliances. But their dials and gadgetry proved incomprehensible, and in what seemed like minutes later the two little chops had charred and decomposed before my eyes. I opened a window to let out the smoke. From the street below rose a sound like an organ grinder's music. It was an ice cream truck rolling along our avenue. A moment later I was carrying two dripping cones back into the apartment. And the last thing I remember about that day was glancing over Yvette's fast dissolving ice cream into our vanity mirror. The light had faded and we appeared to be floating on the velvety surface of her sheets, two frightened children—for that's exactly what we were—intently licking and slurping away our problems.

The next morning Yvette was up before me. Dressed and washed, she sat at the kitchen table writing something in my schoolgirl tablet. Bleary-eyed, I approached her.

"I hope you can read my handwriting," she said.

In neater penmanship than I would ever achieve, she was making out a list.

"All the places Mike likes to hang out in," she explained.

Every other entry ended with "saloon" or "bar."

"Would you," she said, turning around and taking my hand, "would you go out and look for him today?"

"Me?"

"I'd do it myself," she continued, springing up, glancing into the mirror and flopping down on my cot, "but I'm too depressed to move."

Dutifully, I pocketed the list and took to the streets. But you don't search for something you don't want to find and I spent the afternoon in a matinee. Around four, I purchased some wilted daisies and, holding them behind my back, opened our front door.

The entire apartment seemed transformed. The pile of dirty dishes that had accumulated in our sink now sparkled in a cupboard. Corners were vacuumed, the bed was made and three perfect place settings gleamed around the kitchen table. Yvette was seated in front of her vanity mirror, applying lipstick. Her hair was stacked in a tight bouffant, the spaghetti straps of her backless dress flopped over her shoulders and she was wearing her stiletto heels. She watched me walk in.

"Well?" she said. "Well?"

I feigned exhaustion, handed her the pitiful flowers and plopped down on my cot.

"You didn't find him?" She was studying me in the mirror.

"I—"

One by one the daisies spilled from her hands. She got to her feet and began teetering on her heels across the clean but slippery floor, grabbing at furniture for balance. I couldn't look.

"Yvette," I said, amazed at the spontaneous brazenness of my mendacity, "I did everything I could."

From the pile of hair, heels and clothes now laying by my side, her hand reached into the air. For a moment, I was convinced it was going to strangle me. But it groped its way to my pocket and fished out the list. Turning over, Yvette began a frantic roll call, crying out all the names.

"And did you try—?"

"Yes."

"And what about—?"

"Yes."

At the bottom of the list, she stopped for a while to catch her breath. Then, meticulously, she began to shred it. I tried hopelessly to get her to her feet but she seemed intent on turning the paper back into pulp.

"Yvette," I said, "let me at least take off your shoes."

I wanted to get her out of those dangerous heels. Distracted by her now-frenetic shredding, she allowed me to grovel on my hands and knees and unstrap them. Then, silently, one by one, I began to remove bobby pins from her stiff bouffant. I got a rag to wipe away her lipstick, and gently unzipped the dress. I said, "Listen, Yvette, Mike will be back. He'll probably come bouncing through that door any minute."

"Oh, Mike will be back," she said, staring at her pulverized mess. Grabbing a handful, she tossed it into the air—poof—like a cloud. "That," she said, rising to her feet and trodding through the falling scraps to her bed, "that you can be sure of."

14

Mike didn't come back. Every morning Yvette awoke over a precipice of depression and I'd have to coax her from its edge. I'd take out the last of my traveler's checks and she'd wearily crawl into my arms. I'd begin a story-book description of our day. Over those mundane bank notes, now shrinking dangerously low, I'd conjure up the vastness of our possibilities. Yvette never indicated a preference. I had to extract one from her dazed expressions. She wasn't looking too well. Her beautiful cheeks were all puffed up and once, when I fixed us hot fudge sundaes for breakfast, she became extraordinarily ill. I prescribed fresh air and spending as a cure.

But nothing could put her in a better mood. She was either dazed or irritable. I tried to be as cheerful around her as I possibly could, but one day, after lavishing God knows how many gifts upon her, she staggered me with a couple of words.

"Lena," she said, "if you're cheerful around me for another minute, I'm going to go mad." Then she opened her mouth and burst out laughing at me.

I slapped her.

A moment later we were in our bathroom, applying a

cold washcloth to her cheek. I'd have gotten down on my hands and knees to apologize, but Yvette said, "It's I who should apologize, Lena. I'm sorry."

I wanted to do something for her but the only thing I could think of was to lavish another gift on her. I ran to get my money.

"Oh my God," I said. "Yvette, look at this!"

I held up my folder of traveler's checks. Between my fingers sat the thick frayed ends of my check stubs. The metal snap had parted and the flap of the folder opened, revealing two final checks clinging together with static electricity. I said, "Did you see this?"

"I already know," Yvette said.

I sat down on the toilet seat. "Why in God's name didn't you say something, Yvette?"

"What difference would it have made?"

I looked at the two little checks, at the thick worthless stubs. Then I looked at my Yvette. Actually, it wouldn't have made any difference at all. I said, "Oh my God, I'm going to have to leave you now. I'm going to have to get a job."

"Not yet, we've got another errand to run."

"Another errand? Yvette, you're not listening to me."

She wasn't listening. She was examining her cheek in the mirror. So I took my checks along with me and entered her view. I made myself appear haggard. I said, "And what sort of work, what sort of job could I possibly be good for now?"

"Well, certainly not an accountant," Yvette said.

I suddenly burst into tears. I covered my face with my

hands. But I left a gap in my fingers to watch, through my tears and trembling hands, for any tender movement Yvette might make. She gave me her washcloth. I forced my face into it. She daubed my eyes with her embroidered initials. She said, "Don't be a jerk, Lena. I've known for some time. I've got a plan. I've always got a plan."

"What?" I sobbed.

But Yvette didn't answer. She moved a foot or two away but I could sense her body now also racked by tears. I lowered the washcloth. My vision was completely blurred and when I reached out for her, I was an inch or two short. For a moment, I stood awkwardly stroking the air. Then I felt her hand grasp mine. She was walking us to her bed. I willingly complied. We collapsed in a mysterious entanglement of limbs and sheets. For a while, I couldn't tell what belonged to whom. When I looked down we were just bodies. Everywhere I could feel her weight. She continued to cry so I cried too. Between sobs she nuzzled my neck and ears. Once she ran a fingernail along my ribs. Another time she traced a vein up my thigh. I lay absolutely still. Then, ever so bravely, I placed my cheek against her chest. She buried me in her breast.

For me? Was she crying for me this time?

Part Four:
Money and Fathers

15

The next morning Yvette spent the last of my savings on beauty supplies. She lined bottles along the rim of our sink. There was also a vial the color of a crushed orchid, and a wooden bowl with the tongue of a wooden spoon protruding from it.

"And now," Yvette said, "before we visit my father, we've got to dye my hair back to its natural color."

"You're not a redhead?" I said.

"Oh, no," Yvette said, pulling off a lid and releasing an effervescence of shampoo, "I have the same mousy color as you."

She dipped over the sink, laughing. "Wash me," she said.

I took her delicate neck in my hands. Under the force of the water, her hair tapered to the size of her head and she looked ever so small against the bowl of the sink. I wrapped her in a towel. I even sponged her forehead and removed a soapy thread from under her brow.

"And now," Yvette said, "put on these rubber gloves, Lena. We're going to peroxide my hair."

She mixed a solution in the bowl and helped me on with the rubber gloves, and without an inkling of sensation in my fingers I plastered each and every strand, wrapping the whole mess in a towel. While we waited I amused us by chain smoking. With each cigarette, I assumed a different personality. I was a nauseous nurse by the end of the pack. Yvette was in front of the mirror. So I crept up behind her, letting my bleached gloves steal around her form. I said, "Now, little miss, we're going to take off these bandages and see how the plastic surgery came out."

"Lena," Yvette said, "just remove the towel."

But I continued, "We've all wondered, the doctors and I, what shape your little head will take? Will it be round?" I said, unraveling the first loop, "or will it be square? The doctors tried so very hard to remove those nasty horns."

I forked my fingers and pantomimed a snipping scissors. I was delighted with myself. I handed her a hand mirror and suggested she admire herself in profile. Then, in a flurry of motion, I pinched the towel and whipped it from her head.

Framed in elderly white sat Yvette's little features. I was aghast. For a moment I stared into her future—a white and mottled Yvette in front of her vanity mirror. Quickly I found the dye and applied it to her hair until finally, wiping off a sliver of sweat with the heel of my hand, I stood back to examine a darker, almost childlike Yvette turning to me for approval.

"You look beautiful," I told her.

That evening we set her hair in a flip, and the next morning we began the final preparations for visiting her father. Her face was scrubbed clean and the nail polish was removed from her fingers and toes. I found a pair of knee socks tucked away in some drawer, and Yvette dusted off her penny loafers. Finally she pulled out a pleated tunic and a starched white blouse.

"Yvette," I said, "where in God's name did you get that?"

"It's my school uniform."

"Your what?"

"I still have one semester of high school left."

Stunned, I watched her button up the blouse and wiggle into the tunic.

"Dad still likes to think of me as his little girl. It's obnoxious," she said, admiring herself and making last adjustments in the mirror, "but what can I do?" Then she walked up to me, opened her blouse and leaned over. "Smell me," she commanded.

I did, taking a deep whiff of Yvette.

"Any traces of perfume?"

I could barely answer. I shook my head no.

"Thank God," she said, rolling her eyes in relief. She took a step backward and examined me. "Hmmmm, I think we'll have you stay in the background."

She grabbed her purse, rearranged her pleats and I followed her down to the subway, where we caught a train to Nassau and Wall.

16

The financial district was not at all what my tour book had promised. I had anticipated a world that perpetually welcomes heroes. When Yvette and I emerged from the subway, Wall Street looked like any other street, and the young clerks, seen releasing streamers onto generals, astronauts and baseball players in my tour book, pushed their way along, grimacing and indifferent. We entered a tall building and stepped out onto a mezzanine braced by pillars supporting the gigantic dome of its ceiling. Yvette walked up to one, looped her arms around it and leaned over the railing.

"Well, Yvette, can you see your Dad yet?" I asked.

Without turning, she said, "Lena!"

So I looked too. The whole lobby was in motion. Hundreds and hundreds of people were revolving in and out of elevator doors and glass doors with gilded sides and around pillars that ended in planters. From where I stood, gazing over the floor with slight vertigo, the people were reduced to hundreds of miniature heads, like pins stabbed into a revolving lobby.

"Yvette, are you sure you know where you're going?"

She turned and walked over to a winding staircase with

a red carpet. The carpet was worn into shoe shapes, like a slanted dance chart, so that by matching foot for foot, she shuffled on down. But I walked where no feet had trod, right next to the banister, and sank my heels firmly in.

"Hurry up!" Yvette shouted. "We haven't got all day."

At the foot of the staircase, an old man leaned against a cane, and through the space between one bent elbow and the spoke-like divisions of the railing, I saw a part of Yvette's face staring up at me gap-mouthed.

"Was that some kind of joke, Lena? Was that some sort of bridal march?"

"Yvette," I said, "it was vertigo."

I began following her through the lobby. She stopped in front of double glass doors with fingerprints all over them of so many sizes and shapes that the lobby's entire population must have passed through it.

"Well, this is it. This is Dad's office. How do I look?" Yvette asked.

She turned and examined herself in my reaction. I didn't know what to do, so I matched my expression with hers. For a moment we stood opposite each other, licking our lips and fluttering our eyelashes in synchronization. Then she fingered the pleats of her tunic, I smoothed the wrinkles in my pant legs, and we opened the glass doors to the narrow theater of her father's brokerage firm.

From front to back the room was filled with people, but unlike the crowd in the lobby, this crowd was oddly static, squeezed in between rows of theater-like chairs while they watched a gigantic board with columns of shifting numbers. Everybody talked at once. Telephones kept ringing. And the board, with its tumbling numbers on swirling tiles, clattered over the din like chattering teeth.

"Let's stay in back," Yvette said. "Let's wait until Dad's not too busy."

She pointed to her father, a tiny blur next to the board with a telephone dangling from each ear.

"Yvette, maybe we should come back later?"

"When?" Yvette said.

Yvette's father sat slumped in a chair, his head resting against its vinyl back. His eyes were closed and his hands lay on his desk top, curled as if they were about to seize a telephone. Yvette approached him and leaned toward his cheek, and after a second or two of rapid blinking, he opened his eyes and kissed the air beside her. Then, almost imperceptibly, while his lips were still pursed, Yvette whispered something into his ear. Involuntarily I leaned forward to catch her words.

"Please, Dad," Yvette was saying, "can't I have a little more? Something extra this month?"

"I'm sorry," Yvette's father said.

"But Dad—"

"I'm afraid you're not listening, Yvette."

"My God, Dad, it's you who aren't listening."

"This isn't the time or place to discuss this, Yvette.

Out there"—he pointed to the throngs of people—"out there are buyers who've put their faith in me. Take a lesson from them, Yvette."

Suddenly a man with oddly combed hair leaped up beside me.

"Mr. Bigelow!" he shouted.

"Yes," Yvette's father said.

"Mr. Bigelow, look! Look! Cotton's going up!"

"We're buying short today," Yvette's father explained.

"But Mr. Leventhal says," the man said, "Mr. Leventhal says, he says cotton's going up."

"We're buying short today and we're buying pork bellies. I told you you shouldn't come around here, Mr. Pimber."

"But Mr. Leventhal says—" the man pleaded. Then he turned to Mr. Leventhal and as if by command, Mr. Leventhal stood up and shouted, "Look, look, cotton's going up!"

"Cotton's going up," the man agreed.

"Sit down, Mr. Pimber," Yvette's father insisted.

Mr. Pimber sat down. He said, "I don't even know what buying short means."

"As you can see," Yvette's father continued, lowering his voice, "I already have my hands full."

"But what about me, Dad?"

"You?"

For several seconds he looked at his daughter as if trying to recall exactly who she was. Then he took out his bill-fold.

"It's against my principles," he said, reaching inside.

Money

Stacks of brilliantly colored credit cards toppled onto his desk. "Your stepmother and I had been saving this for your birthday"—and he thumbed through the stacks, removing a white, sealed envelope, which he handed to her.

"Well?" he said.

Yvette tore open the envelope and peered inside.

"Don't I even hear a thank you?"

"Yeah, Dad," Yvette said, "thanks a lot." She turned and began walking briskly toward the rear of the theater. I caught up with her in the last aisle.

"But I haven't met your father."

"Let's go," Yvette said.

In the subway, we rode in absolute silence. I kept telling myself, Boy, are we going to be lucky from here on in. A corner of the white envelope protruded from Yvette's pocket, and when we changed trains I used it as a beacon to guide me, thinking, This is it. This is luck. At our apartment, I finally couldn't stand it any longer and I tried to embrace Yvette and the envelope in the doorway.

"Oh, I'll just bet my bottom dollar, we're in for a spell of luck," I said.

"You already have," Yvette said.

She pinched open the envelope and removed a slip of paper. It was a gift certificate for another appliance.

17

Yvette closed all the blinds and spent the afternoon watching cartoons with the volume off. I paced nervously back and forth. The white envelope lay crumpled by Yvette's side. Finally, in a desperate effort to break the silence, I sat down next to her and began simulating the missing sound of the television set. Placing my lips next to her ear, I made guttural noises, each matching some cartoon machination. When a miniature duck got flattened by a steam roller, I hissed. But when the duck walked out a window onto thin air and kept walking, I suddenly felt dreadful.

"Maybe we should turn off the television set and talk for a while," I suggested.

She shook her head no.

"Yvette, I'm miserable," I said.

She ignored me.

"Please let me turn that thing off. We've got to talk."

But Yvette motioned me to stay away from the television set. She clenched a fist and pointed to the spot where I sat. So I watched the duck scramble into a telephone booth. Removing a glove, its human fingers dialed and the screen split and another, older duck with spectacles answered.

I kidded, "Hey, Dad, could you send money?"

"Now," Yvette said, "now you can turn the television set off, Lena."

I stretched over Yvette, fumbling for the dials. I turned one and tightened another and pulled frantically on a third. It came off in my hands. The duck, who was flashing around the perimeter of the screen, faded away into darkness. Only the steady hum of the television set remained. I turned to Yvette, holding up the unattached dial for her to see, then maneuvered myself behind the bureau searching for the plug. A dozen cords dangled from the socket. Wires were crossed and plugs extended out from one another.

"Yvette, you've got to give me a clue."

But Yvette was crying. The hum of the television set muffled her sobs as she sat in the blue light of the cathode tube, gently quivering. I grabbed all the wires and pulled. The room went dark.

"Yvette, this is nothing." I removed a stray cord from around my ankle. "It'll only cost pennies to repair."

"I'm pregnant," Yvette said.

I groped my way to her side.

"Are you sure?"

"Absolutely."

"How did it happen?"

"Use your brains, Lena."

"When?"

"What difference does it make?"

Actually, it didn't make any difference at all.

"Lena," Yvette whispered, "I hate the dark."

So I worked my way over to the windows and opened a blind. I stood there for a moment gazing out. I think I was amazed that the world hadn't abruptly changed, that everything remained exactly as before. That our neighbors still calmly chewed their dinners across the way. That a little boy and girl cared enough about a half-flattened ball to bicker over its ownership. That a man stood dejected after attempting to hail several taxicabs. Then I snapped open the other blind and returned to Yvette's side.

Part Five:
Credit

18

I climbed off my seat and out through the doors of the subway, holding Yvette's heavy television and wondering how I held it so delicately. I'd had the dial fixed. Yvette was supposed to meet me at the station. An old man sat on a wooden bench nervously counting his change on the green slabs.

"Sir," I asked, "do those steps lead up to Lexington Avenue?"

But he ignored me. He was stacking quarters on his knees.

"Sir?"

"I've got arthritis," he said.

"Oh, I'm sorry. I didn't know arthritis affects hearing."

"I've got arthritis," he said, trying to show me his crooked hands, "and I think, I think I've dropped a quarter."

"A quarter?" I was looking for Yvette, my eyes fixed on the stairwell.

"Yes," he said, shoving a handful of quarters in front of my eyes, "I think I'm one short."

"Maybe you spent it," I suggested, "maybe you bought cigarettes with it?"

"No," he said, "I don't smoke. I've got arthritis."

174

"I'm sorry," I said. A large crowd was moving down the stairwell but a hanging sign hid their heads so I searched for Yvette's shoes. Then their shoes trampled behind the token counter so I looked for Yvette's jacket.

"Perhaps," he said, tugging on my pant leg, "perhaps you could look for my quarter."

"I'm sorry, I'm already looking for something."

"Perhaps," he said, "perhaps we could switch what we're looking for."

So I described Yvette and unhooked his fingers from my pant leg, got down on my hands and knees and started looking for his quarter. He lifted up his feet for me to look under his shoes. He said, "Look how nimble you are!"

My legs were straddling the television set while my fingers slid under his shoes. He asked, still with his feet in the air, "How old are you?"

I don't know why but I lied, "Eighteen, sir."

"My God," he said.

I said, "You see Yvette?"

"My God," he said, "my eyes aren't what they used to be."

"Terrific," I said.

"You found my quarter?"

"No, not yet."

He put his feet down while I wedged myself under the bench. My fingers began feeling around the shadow cast by the television. Then they crawled over to the bench's iron legs and poked between the grooves. Suddenly one finger touched plastic. It was Yvette's shoes.

"Lena, for God's sake, what are you doing?"

"Looking for a quarter."

"A quarter?" Yvette said. "A quarter? What difference does a quarter make now?"

"It's his," I said, pointing up at the old man.

"Lena, for God's sake, just give the man a quarter."

I gave the man a quarter.

"This isn't my quarter," he said.

"What difference does it make?" Yvette said.

She leaned over and scooped up the television set and we carried it back to our apartment. Even before we reached the top landing, I sensed something was wrong. Our door had been left ajar. Yvette nudged it open with her shoulder. I couldn't believe what I saw. Propped up with pillows, Mike was sprawled across *our* bed. I said, "What are you doing here?"

"Yvette phoned me at my parents' house on Long Island."

"You what?" I said, turning to Yvette.

"She's pregnant," Mike said.

"I know!"

"It seems I'm the last to know."

Yvette carried the television set over to the bed and began tearing off the brown wrapping paper. I sat down next to Mike. Behind us, from a window, an oblong of sunlight cast three waxen shadows, the color of muddy ice, on the now unveiled screen.

"Well, how did it happen?" Mike asked.

"You're beginning to sound like Lena," Yvette said.

She inspected the dial and began fidgeting with the antenna.

"I just asked you a simple question, Yvette. Could you please stop fooling around with that thing?"

"No."

"What am I going to do?" Mike asked me.

I kept my suggestions to myself.

"When I'm around," Mike continued, "I'd like a little attention."

"When I'm around," Yvette mimicked, "I'd like a little attention."

She began polishing the screen with her sleeve.

"Yvette, I've just spent an hour on the train. If you're not going to talk to me then why did you call?"

"Beats me," Yvette said.

She asked me to bring her a clean rag.

"Forget the TV!" Mike said, "just put it away!"

He reached over to grab it.

"Don't touch it," Yvette said. "It was a present from Dad, along with everything else in here. And that makes it mine."

"And I suppose you own the baby too," Mike said.

"No," Yvette said, "because outside of here where we sometimes went but not enough, *you* own the other half. And that's why I called!"

Mike pointed to the TV.

"That's your real child, Yvette, and thank God it's not half mine."

Then he left, slamming the door behind him.

Yvette sat down on the bed. "I think he likes being a father, don't you?"

She broke into a soundless laugh. She laughed so hard she had to put her head between her legs. Suddenly, her eyes, balanced in the space between her knees, turned white. It looked like milk was poured into them.

"Are you all right?" I asked.

"Oh God," Yvette said, "what am I going to do?"

I walked over to the bed and lay down next to her. Now and then I could hear a car swish softly by. I leaned my mouth by her ear.

"I've got a wonderful idea. Forget about Mike, get your father to pay for an abortion and you and I can live together just like we have been."

She said softly, "Don't be an idiot, Lena."

"Idiot?"

"Listen, Mike is my whole life, and my father, let me tell you about my father, he's got to continue being our meal ticket."

"I'll . . . I'll get a job."

"Do you really think I could live on your salary? Besides, why do you think I had you move in in the first place? Why not just live with Mike? Didn't it ever occur to you that my father would no longer be a meal ticket if he knew that Mike was my whole life?"

It never had occurred to me, but I said, "Of course."

She rolled over and faced me and instantly my eyelids felt wet. She tried to take my hand. I recoiled from her grasp.

"Well," she said, "we haven't got much time left."

"We, Yvette?"

"Lena, if I can't depend on you now, if after these three months of our living like this, with you on the cot, with you on the cot watching me like entertainment—"

"Yvette," I lied, "I never looked."

Eventually Yvette rocked herself to sleep, but I couldn't get comfortable. My lids were too heavy to keep open, yet when I closed them my breath became short. So I went to my cot and lay down, blinking and smoking cigarettes. But smoking without watching is pleasureless. I mashed out my cigarette and shut my lids. In the near blackness I tried to re-create the image of Yvette's face—brow, nose, lips, chin. The Yvette who assembled before me was as objective as a police sketch. I think I believed if I could just see her clearly everything would fall into focus. And for several seconds I almost had her pinned to the underside of my lids. Then, feature by feature, she slowly dissolved and I saw only black and rudimentary colors in rudimentary patterns. I lay there thinking, This is my life. It was so simple. . . . A rudimentary life for a rudimentary fool. Faintly, I heard a gap in the traffic sounds outside. An auto horn said, Fool.

19

From beneath the covers I awoke to the sound of metal; I opened my eyes and lifted the sheets. I was slightly disoriented, I hadn't slept on my cot in weeks. All around the apartment were piles of appliances, some I'd never seen before—popcorn poppers, ice makers, orange juice squeezers. Yvette was sitting on the window sill, cleaning a percolator. The blinds, not completely shut, filtered dim strokes of still light. They hung like soap on her appliances.

She looked down at me and stopped polishing.

"If we're going to entice anyone, Lena, most of all pawnbrokers, you'll need to put on something that makes you look older, something low-cut." Then she began polishing again, adding, "By the way, did you have a good rest, by yourself and everything?"

"Yvette," I said, "get your father to pay. I am not selling myself."

"Did I say that?" Yvette said. "Did I? I said try and look a little older, that's what I said. You are naive, Lena."

Then she got up, went to a closet, and tossed me a coat hanger with a black dress slung over it.

"I cannot believe this," I said.

"Believe it," Yvette said. She picked up the coat hanger. "Would you like to try it? Would you? It would save a lot of money on the abortion, Lena."

I fixed my eyes on the spot where the metal hooked. I said, "Get your father to pay."

She said, "Father is paying. These, as you'll remember"—and she wrapped an electric cord around her neck—"are presents from my father."

I said, "It seems to me it would have been a lot simpler to give you the money."

"This is money. Here," she said, tossing me a rag, "polish."

So I began cleaning on the television set.

"Don't bother," Yvette said, "that's going to be hidden in the basement in case Mike shows up while we're out. Do you really think I'd lie around after the abortion without any comforts? I just want him to see how much I'm suffering."

Then she handed me the disassembled pieces of a waffle iron and as I polished them, she explained how surfaces were the most viable commodity we had to pawn.

20

It was Yvette and I; or Yvette and the box with the stereo and I and the toaster; or, as Yvette said, Yvette and the only-used-once-and-that-is-it stereo and I and the never-been-opened-because-none-of-us-like-our-bread-charred toaster.

She was walking several feet in front of me. "Make it look like we are separate," Yvette told me. "If we are separate, we are twice as many or twice as lucky."

So we walked separately. But I didn't believe it mattered, because when you see one pigeon you know others are around. Yvette entered a pawn shop while I waited outside. The sun was almost vertical and the glare of the asphalt made my eyes tear. I leaned into the window, staring at the cool dark interior. Jewelry and appliances with patches of chrome harmonized vibrantly in the reflective windowpane. I watched that for a while until my eyes focused and the foreground dissipated like smoke. Then I looked more intently and saw Yvette standing next to a counter fronted by a wire cage. And as I kept watching, I could feel the sun beat down against the glass and drain all the city noise out of my ears. So it was me,

alone, watching like a movie Yvette and the pawnbro-
ker. Like the silent cinema.

And as in the silent cinema, each of Yvette's urgent
hand gestures, the exaggerated bemusement of the pawn-
broker's face, took on an air of melodrama. Only the
money exchange, with its subdued movements and bitter
facial expressions, reminded me of sound, and from where
I stood I could almost hear the crispness of dollar bill on
dollar bill.

Yvette pushed open the door. She said, "That beast
took me."

"How much?"

"Twenty-five dollars, twenty-five lousy, stinking dollars."

I entered the next pawnshop.

I said to myself, "This is not mysterious, this is like a
grocery store." Hand-worn possessions were stacked shelf
after shelf, as in a cupboard without walls, arranged in a
time sequence and labeled not by item but by dust. I said
to myself, "This is not like a grocery store, this is like a
public attic."

Behind the counter sat the broker. A black man was
dangling a silver watch before him.

"Hey, old man," the black man said, "what are you
going to give me?"

"A dollar."

"A dollar? I can't believe this"—the black man held his
chin and rocked—"no, I can't believe this."

"Believe this," the broker said. "I'll give you a dollar."

"No," the black man said, "this watch is worth over twenty. You give me five."

"I'll give you nothing," the broker said.

"But you have got to," the black man said.

"I've got to nothing! I'll give you nothing!"

"Silver," the black man said.

"You cannot sell me on silver. You cannot sell me on anything.'"

"Silver, fine, fine silver. You are a fool, Jew."

"Let me see it," the broker said.

The black man fingered it more delicately. "Give me five bucks."

"Give me give me give me. Forget it, I'll give you nothing. Get your black face out of here."

"Give me a couple of bucks." The black man wrapped his fingers through the wire cage. "Old man, give me two dollars."

The broker raised his hands as if the black man had a weapon.

"Thief," he said, and handed him two dollars.

"Old man, give me another fifty cents."

The broker lowered his hands and dismissed the black man with a gesture like flapping. Then he pointed to me, saying, "Okay. You."

I said, "Me?" I lifted the box with the toaster onto the counter.

"How much do you want for that stuff?"

"Twenty," I said.

"Ten," he said.

"Sold," I said.

Money

The broker slowly scrawled out a ticket and handed me my money, a single bill. On the street, Yvette was standing in the shade of an awning and as I approached her, I noticed water glistening along her upper lip. She said, "How much?"

"Yvette, I couldn't help it." I unlatched my purse to show her the ten-dollar bill.

She didn't say anything, just stared at the bill. So, gently, I handed it to her, folding her fingers around it.

"Yvette," I said, "what should we do now?"

"Nothing."

"Nothing? Yvette, this won't even pay for your cab fare."

"I thought you didn't approve of taking cabs."

"Yvette, that's not the point," I whispered. "What about the abortion?"

"It'll get taken care of!"

Then she turned and began walking down the block. I went to the opposite corner and down the steps of the subway. I didn't look back. The sun disappeared while I blinked. It was as if my eyes were still closed, yet I saw the sparkle of a shiny token and a passing watch band. I sat down on a bench until my eyes were able to see duller details. Then I walked over to a concession stand and ordered a Coke. I drank it and chewed on the ice and, when the ice had melted, I drank the bitter after-water.

21

When I returned, Yvette was already in her bathrobe, sprawled on my cot with the telephone cord tangled around her legs. The receiver lay on the empty bureau. And as I shut the door I heard, faintly, over Yvette's steady sighs, the electrical thump of a busy signal.

"Mike's not at any of the bars. Mike's not at his parents'. Mike's disappeared for good this time," Yvette sighed.

I walked over to the unhooked receiver and cradled it in my palm.

"Who are you phoning?"

"His nonstop talking sister. She's just like him. He sometimes stays with her."

"Then maybe it's Mike on the line. Maybe he's talking to someone?"

"Who?" Yvette said.

"Good God, Yvette, how am I supposed to know?"

"No," she sighed, tossing slightly, "he's disappeared for good this time."

"Yvette," I said, sitting down beside her. I stroked her forehead, coiling and uncoiling her damp threads of hair. "Yvette, don't be so melodramatic, Mike's probably—" But she slipped out from between my fingers, leaving my hands awkwardly dangling, and began tossing again. So I said, "Yvette, don't be so melodramatic about him. It's annoying."

"Annoying?" Yvette said. "Annoying?" Limb by limb, she raised herself up. A queer look came over her features as she crawled over and began hovering in the space above me. "Annoying?" she said, focusing down on me. "Without Mike, Lena, I feel like a bug. No wonder I'm annoying!"

I said, "Yvette, don't look at me that way, it's not my problem. It once was my problem but I can't take it any longer. God only knows he certainly didn't show you much love."

For a moment I was tempted to add, Not as much love as I could have shown.

"He'd better come back," Yvette said, "because if he doesn't I will have the baby and—"

"And what?" I said. "And what?"

She thought about it for a moment.

"I will have the baby and I will name the baby Mike. And when the baby grows old enough, we will find Mike and follow him around until he goes insane and kills the baby."

"After all this, Yvette, you have the baby and I'll kill all three of you," I said.

But Yvette wasn't listening. She said, "Good, now I've got a plan. I will work on making Mike insane."

I said, "Mike is already insane and you are driving *me* insane with your insanity."

"I know, I know," she said. "You've been my only source
of clear thinking and I am grateful."

"Do you want me to try and find Mike again?"

"Do you really think you can? Do you really think you
can? Remember, it's almost like your own baby."

"Sure," I said, "that's just what I'm thinking about, my
share of the baby."

Yvette insisted on sleeping with her light on. Around
dawn, I finally extinguished it. Yvette stirred. Quietly I
put on a pair of her slippers and padded over to the alarm
clock. I set it for two and scrawled a note. I WILL SEE
YOU AT THE DOCTOR'S AT THREE. MAYBE WITH MIKE.
Then I got dressed and, needing some change for my
bus fare, peered into the envelope Yvette's father had
given her. She kept the pawnshop money inside it. I
dumped it on the bureau. Several bills fell out along with
the gift certificate. I pocketed five dollars.

At a drugstore I got change for the bus. I put the
quarters in my pants pocket and stuffed the bills under a
flap on my shirt. And after that, wherever I walked, the
quarters rattling in my pocket sounded as if a dog was
following me. The sound of prosperity, I said to myself.

I checked Mike's sister's apartment but nobody was
home. I went to some of the bars I remembered from
Yvette's list. I was too young to enter so I stood by their
doors tapping clients on the shoulders. Nobody had seen
Mike. Next I got on a bus and went up and down the
streets, but I couldn't see anything except the tops of

heads. I got off around midtown and phoned Yvette.

I said, "Yvette, you go on without me."

"You haven't found Mike?"

"No, you go on without me, and I'll meet you there."

She read me the doctor's address and I wrote it on a dollar bill. Then I hung up and walked over to a park bench and sat down. It was past one and the heat had accumulated in layers; whenever I looked up, it seemed as if I was looking through water. I leaned my neck directly against a baking pole of dull iron. It felt like a match was put to my skin and my arms flew out uncontrollably, scraping a hand on the wooden slats of the bench. It started bleeding so I sucked on it. Just then, peering out of the gaps between my fingers, I saw two boys approaching. Frazzled and haphazard—but strangely haphazard, self-consciously relaxed; that is how they approached, their arms dangling, one thumb looped in a belt knotch.

The first one walked over and I thought he might ask the time but he didn't say anything. He just fumbled a while in his pants pocket while the other stood nervously behind him.

"You got any spare change?" he finally asked.

I said, fixing to leave, "Are you kidding me?"

But he sat down extremely close to me while the second one put his foot on the bench.

"Now, Lance, now," the second one said.

The first one leaned over and collared me. "You better pay up," he whispered.

"How much do you want?"

"Is she kidding you?" the second one asked the first.

"Are you kidding us?" the first one said.

"Do I look like I'm kidding?"

"She's just stalling, Lance."

"Is that what you're doing, girl?" the first one asked.

"No, I'm not stalling," I said. "As a matter of fact, I'm in a hurry. Well, what is it you want?"

"Hey, Lance," the second one said, "she wants to know what we want."

"We want all your money," Lance said. Then he turned to the second one. "I can't believe I'm saying this, give me all your money. Can you believe this?"

I reached into my pants pocket and pulled out the quarters.

"Here," I said, "that's all there is." I held out the change for them to see.

"There's not even a dollar there," the second one said. "Lance, what are we going to do?"

"We're going to search her pockets. Girl, let me see what you got hidden in those pockets."

He searched my pockets and pulled out the three dollars.

"What else you got hidden in there?"

"Nothing," I said. Then I pointed to the dollar bill with the address written on it. "May I borrow that for a few minutes?"

"She's crazy, Lance. Do something."

"Okay, girl," Lance said, "take off those shoes."

"Are you kidding me?" I said.

"I said," Lance said, "take off them shoes."

I took off my shoes. My feet felt like hands on the pavement.

"Well, check her shoes," Lance said.

The second one bent over and fumbled around in my shoes.

"They clean, Lance."

"See?" I said.

Then they left and I stooped over to replace my shoes. There was a green splinter from the bench in my left thumb so I balled the laces with my right hand and shoved them under my heels. Suddenly, while my head was still level with my shoes, I began whistling. I couldn't stop myself. I said, "Oh, this is so poor, this is so downtrodden."

I walked miserably home.

Yvette hadn't returned so I left the door ajar and went into the bathroom. I checked the medicine cabinet for a safety pin but I couldn't find one, so I used my teeth to dig out the splinter. Then I ran cold water over my thumb and dried it on my shirt. I wrapped it in toilet paper and lay down on my cot. And with my thumb tucked securely between my thighs, I dozed off.

22

Is that you?" I said. I was lying on my cot trying to rub the sleep out of my eyes. The door was still ajar. Along the hallway I could hear her walking. She walked as if she were heavier.

"Yvette," I said, "are you back already?"

"Don't bother me now!"

I could still hear her toiling up the staircase so I went to look out the door. The hallway was pitch black. I groped for the light switch.

"Why didn't you call me?" I said.

"Don't bother me now!"

She was carrying the television up from the basement, her two pale arms wrapped around the screen, a crescent of face protruding between the antenna. I wanted to say, Are you crazy? but I couldn't say anything. I just stood there. Then the television slipped from her grasp and Yvette was toppling backwards. I ran down the stairs.

"Are you crazy?" I said.

When I got there, she was doubled over, clinging to the banister.

"What did you go and do this for?" But it was like

scolding a child after it had been hit by a car. Then I
saw she was bleeding.

"Can you walk?" I asked softly.

She shook her head no.

"Don't you want to try?"

"Poor Lena," Yvette said.

"You get up and try to walk," I said. But she kept saying, "Poor Lena, poor Lena."

"What did you say that for?"

"Poor Lena," she said.

"Shut up or I'll leave you here, Yvette."

I got her to sit up and I cradled her in my arms.

"What did you do this for?" I asked. "Now what am I
going to do?"

I rocked her and stroked her wet thighs. My fingers
became sticky with blood. I said, "It's all right, don't worry
about a thing."

Then I plugged up her ears with my fingers so she
couldn't hear the panic in my voice, and I shouted for
the landlady.

"Please!" I said. "Call an ambulance!"

When I pulled my fingers out of Yvette's ears, the ear
holes were red. The landlady stood transfixed in front of
us.

"You've got to hurry," I said.

She turned but she couldn't take her eyes off of Yvette.
Then she started moving down the stairwell, her eyes
bouncing off the steps and Yvette. When I heard her
door slam beneath us, I plugged up Yvette's ears again
and waited for the siren.

* * *

The first one said, "Who are you?"

I said, "Me? I'm just her roommate."

The second one said, "Did you know she had an abortion?"

"Yes," I said. "It would be peculiar if I didn't."

They had Yvette's legs propped up on the banister, a white sheet draped over them.

"Well," the second one said, "she's stopped bleeding."

"Thank God," I said.

They lifted her onto the stretcher. Then the first one examined her ears.

"Jesus, I think she's bleeding at the head."

"No," I explained, "that's where I put my fingers." I showed them my hands.

"Does she have relatives?" the second one asked.

"Yes, of course."

"Go call them."

So I climbed back up the steps and when I got to the shattered television set, I stooped over and picked it up and carried it to her bureau, adjusting the antenna as if it mattered.

After I called Yvette's father I checked my pockets for money but, of course, they were empty. Then I checked the white envelope. The gift certificate was still inside but the money was gone. Somehow, I couldn't get myself to take the gift certificate. So I got down on my hands and knees and began crawling under the table where we'd kept our purses, my fingers feeling for lost change. Suddenly, from behind a table leg, my face leaped into the vanity mirror. It looked flat and white as I examined it. I said aloud to myself, "Who's that fool in the mirror?" Then I reached up and got a candy bar out of my purse and watched myself eat it in the mirror. Instantly, I remembered the image of Yvette and me devouring our ice cream cones. "Fool," I said between swallows, "I'll be damned, I've been taken." When the candy bar was gone I took out a cigarette. I watched myself smoke. Eventually the smoke sealed my flat head and the table leg. The table leg and I just sat in her vanity mirror. I said to myself, "We're buddies, you and I, eh?"

I reached over for the telephone and watched myself dial in the mirror. Then I watched my mouth say into the telephone, "Yes, I need information."

It was a woman's voice. It put me on hold. I sat on hold and smoked another cigarette. When the voice said, "Yes?" I mashed out the cigarette.

"I need some information about a girl who has just been admitted." Then I gave Yvette's name.

"Are you a relative?"

"The patient's mother."

"Oh, pardon me, you sounded so young."

"Can I help it if I sound young?"

"No," the voice said. "Your husband is here. Your daughter is going to be just fine. We'll be keeping her here for the night but it's only a precaution. Her fiancé is in there with her now."

SMALL CLAIMS

I hung up with my finger and left the telephone unhooked. I wrapped the wire around my neck and pulled.
I saw my head swell in the mirror. I said to myself, "Fool."

Then I got up and started packing. Yvette had long
ago talked me into throwing away my suitcase, so I folded
up my shirts and slacks and stuffed them into a grocery
bag. I put my little schoolgirl tablet on top of that. Then
I wrapped up my toothbrush and some leftover aspirins
in toilet paper and stuffed the wad into my extra shoes.
I put those in a pillowcase, checked to make sure I still
had my tour book and began looking around for anything else I might have forgotten. The snapshot of me
on top of the Empire State Building was still taped above
my cot. I stopped for a moment, anticipating a wave of
nostalgia, but I didn't feel a thing. I couldn't even remember why I'd had it taken. I simply plucked it from the
wall and added it to the collection of photographs adorn-
ing the edges of Yvette's vanity. Then I sat down and
wildly began applying make-up. When I no longer recognized myself I stopped. I checked the closets one last
time, fingering all the pockets of Yvette's clothes. In a
jacket, I found twenty-six cents. I pocketed it.

I walked several blocks without noticing in which direction I was going. Above me, a cafe sign blinked scarlet
and orange neon. Its on-again, off-again was far more
sensuous than its colors, and the smell of human sweat,
now more delicious than bacon frying, made my tongue
swell.

I sat down at the counter, ordering a cup of coffee.
The waitress said, "What are you doing out at this hour?

By yourself and everything. This ain't a walking neighborhood."

She poured my coffee and it smelled sweet, although I hadn't added any sugar.

"Do you have anything fresher?"

"Only me!" She let out a hideous laugh. I could see her breath stir the coffee.

"Well, honey?" she said.

"Well honey what?"

"What are you doing out at this hour?"

"Why do you want to know?"

"Honey," she said, "I get in here around eight in the morning. I don't get off my feet except for lunch. All that comes in here looks the same as me or worse. How many things do you think I can talk about with those same old faces coming in here day in and day out. A pretty young thing walks in here well past midnight and I says to myself, I says, 'Jesus, Marge, maybe you'll have something new to tell those same old faces in the morning.' Now, honey, can you blame me?"

I said, "No, I can't blame you."

"Well?" she said. "Well?"

"I have nowhere else to go."

"Honey," she said, "if that's all you got going for you as troubles, I ain't got nothing to report."

ABOUT THE AUTHOR

Jill Ciment was born in Montreal, Canada. *Small Claims* is her first collection of stories. She lives in New York City and is at work on a novel.